The Lost Boys from
Longwood

*What Hides Behind the Walls
of a Facility Housing Wards
of the Stated with a Juvenile
Record. True Stories.*

J. C. Pater

© 2019 J. C. Pater

All rights reserved. No portion of this book may be reproduced in any form without permission from the publisher, except as permitted by U.S. copyright law.

TABLE OF CONTENTS

INTRODUCTION V

CHAPTER ONE
  » Maurice................................... 1

CHAPTER TWO
  » Young and Deadly 8

CHAPTER THREE
  » Josh 13

CHAPTER FOUR
  » Angels from the Gridiron and Manicured
    Monsters................................. 19

CHAPTER FIVE
  » Stick Shift 26

CHAPTER SIX
  » ¡Yo Amo México!.......................... 30

CHAPTER SEVEN
  » Of Love, Bolts, and Monopoly Games....... 37

CHAPTER EIGHT
  » Born Male, Poor, and Black 44

CHAPTER NINE
  » Anything Can Be a Weapon 51

CHAPTER TEN
  » LGBT 57

CHAPTER ELEVEN
  » Diagnosis: Damaged Beyond Repair 65

CHAPTER TWELVE
  » See No Evil 72

CHAPTER THIRTEEN
  » How to Torment a Teacher 79

CHAPTER FOURTEEN
  » Cash Cow 86

CHAPTER FIFTEEN
  » The End 93

AUTHOR'S NOTE   98

NOTES   101

INTRODUCTION

Under the supervision of Child Protective Services, close to sixty thousand American children are currently housed in group homes or residential facilities. This number represents thirteen percent of the entire foster care population in the United States. Depending on whom you ask, group homes are described either as a reasonable housing option for youngsters who would be challenging to place in foster homes, or as an aberration harboring violence, corruption, and abuse.

In recent years, California has conducted research of the institutionalized care for the youth referred by the Child Protective Services[1]. The study recognized a wide variety of residential programs ranging from family-style group homes and substance abuse centers to locked facilities for sexual offenders and other juvenile criminals. Institutions housing wards of the states varied based on their function, target population, length of stay, level of restrictiveness, and approach to treatment. The study analyzed several treatment models relevant to group care and compared outcomes such as moral judgment, social skills, and recidivism. The researchers noted that all group care models are in early developmental stages, and that there is insufficient data to offer recommendations on a specific approach.

A lot of information on residential facilities for youth in care also came from news reports, and these reports contained a very different verbiage from that of the carefully selected formal speech of the studies. *Chicago Tribune*, for example, published a series of articles depicting group homes and residential facilities for wards of the state in Illinois[2]. In essence, they were described as chaos, pandemonium, and a breeding ground for sexual exploitation. The newspaper analyzed three years of reports and found out that during that time, almost thirty thousand children ran away from the facilities. On average, there were twenty-seven escapes per day, and some runaways were as young as ten. Many of these children were never found.

During the same three-year period, there were over four hundred reports alleging sexual assault, and more than a thousand reports claiming physical abuse. Children placed in group homes and residential facilities were routinely losing basic privileges and freedoms: they were often medicated to the point of having visible side effects, they were surrounded by violence, and forced or coerced into prostitution. When the time came for these kids to leave their group homes and residential facilities, they were more damaged than when they came. And all of this came with a price tag of about three hundred fifty dollars per child per day paid by the Illinois taxpayers.

Another powerful voice came from the *Miami Herald* and focused on the recipients of the juvenile justice system. The Florida newspaper described institutions that were overseen either by the local governments or by private entities[3]. The articles exposed inadequate supervision and frequent use of excessive force while restraining children in crisis: a child's head was plunged into a toilet while another child was assaulted with a broomstick, and an employee hired to protect the youth flung a plastic chair into the face of an eighth-grader with special needs who was in a wheelchair. On average, in the fiscal year 2016, a youth in a juvenile detention center was physically restrained three and a half times every day. Violence was routinely used to control young people who were supposed to be taught how to resolve conflicts without resorting to violence.

These and other reports triggered action by some members of the US Congress to introduce legislation that would better regulate group homes and residential facilities for wards of the states. Most bills did not pass and nothing changed. Nobody seems to have an idea of how to fix the broken system of the residential care for youth in care of the states.

What is life really like in residential facilities for wards of the states? Is the society failing this vulnerable population while state governments are hiding behind a *see no evil, hear no evil* approach?

I hope that the reader will find some answers in the pages of this book. "The Lost Boys from Longwood: What Hides Behind the Walls of a Facility Housing Wards of the Stated with a Juvenile Record" is an account of real events which took place in a residential facility in the Chicago area. Incidents described in this book are sometimes shocking and disturbing, other times comical and grotesque, yet always factual. This book gives a voice to youngsters who were victims of neglect, abuse, and - at times – unimaginable torment which turned some of them into abusers. It seeks to open eyes, and it asks for understanding.

This is what is hiding behind the thick curtain of children privacy laws, put in place to theoretically protect children, but often used to hide corruption, abuse, and neglect.

CHAPTER ONE

Maurice

Maurice was a Katrina survivor. Hurricane Katrina, which hit the Gulf Coast of the United States in 2005, killed at least 1,245 people, breached fifty-three levees that were supposed to protect the city of New Orleans, and caused incalculable damage. Over a million people were displaced, and the population of New Orleans fell from 484,674 to 230,172. Maurice's mother was among the displaced.

Maurice's mom was relocated to Chicago. She was alone, traumatized, and with two children in tow - Maurice and his little brother, at that time just a toddler. When the hurricane hit, Maurice was twelve, which made him old enough to be in shock but too young to know how to deal with it. To his defense, few people knew how to act, including his mother. Life simply does not prepare you for such an extreme disaster. Soon after TV spotlights moved on to the next big story, Maurice's mother started falling apart. She did not know how to handle being removed from everything and everyone she knew. She did not know where to go for help. She was not capable of taking care of her little family.

This is how Maurice became a street child. It was not exactly his choice but he did what he had to do to survive. By the time he turned fifteen, Maurice was taking care of himself. He was romancing a local street gang but, as an outsider, he never gained their full trust. He only did occasional errands for the gang and supplemented that income with minor thefts, panhandling, and other forms of *hustling*. Sometimes, Maurice was even able to bring money home to his mom, now a full-blown drug addict, and to his little brother. Until, one day, Maurice ran out of luck. He was caught stealing, arrested, and turned over to DCFS, the Illinois Department of Children & Family Services. He spent time in a Juvenile Detention Center but after a while, the people in charge eventually sent him to Longwood.

Longwood Treatment Center was a residential facility for troubled youth and juvenile sexual offenders, housing around sixty adolescent males. They were all wards of the state or, to use the politically correct euphemism, youth-in-care of the state. Longwood was a semi-locked facility, not exactly a prison but operating based on the assurance that the boys placed there would not be able to run away. They were not allowed to leave without adult supervision.

The facility, spreading over several secluded acres, was hidden among woods and swamps on a far suburb of Chicago, forty plus miles north of the city. All the residents were boys, mostly between the ages of fourteen and eighteen. A small contingent of older high school graduates resided in a trailer separated from the mail buildings.

Longwood's residents belonged to three major groups: sexual offenders, gangbangers, and the ones who had nowhere to go because no foster home would accept them. Maurice, not really a full-fledged banger, belonged to that third group. A fifteen-year-old African American male with an open criminal case is not a good candidate for a foster home. Giving him back to a permanently stoned mom was not a viable option. When his shoplifting charges were dismissed – juvenile courts were way too busy to deal with petty thefts – Maurice, still a minor and still with nowhere to go, joined the boys permanently warehoused at Longwood.

During his time there, Maurice was never a popular kid. He was different. He spoke with that strange Louisiana accent with its melodious diction. Due to his Southern charm, or maybe because he grew up in a family with an autocratic grandmother and an army of uncles, cousins, and aunts, he was remarkably polite. Most other boys, whose lives were all about vulgarity and violence, found him annoying. From time to time, Maurice was their punching bag. Gang affiliations that usually transfer to the residential facilities for inner city kids were not strong enough to protect him. At Longwood, Maurice had no friends.

To Maurice, his popularity at Longwood did not matter. He simply could not stand Illinois. He never adjusted to the Midwest. He was a true son of the South - a New Orleans native who did not belong up North. During the never-ending Chicago winters, locked in a gloomy old building housing wards of the state, Maurice would sit on the floor with his back to the wall. He wrapped himself in an ugly, colorless blanket and sat with a blank expression on his face. He was dreaming about home.

Maurice's grandmother and his sizable extended family in Louisiana were making continuous efforts to bring Maurice back, but they were getting nowhere. They were sent from one bureaucrat to another, provided with contradictory or confusing information, and cumulatively spending countless hours on hold. Little did they know about the anti-reciprocal approach practiced by the child welfare agencies in different states. Even if the state level agencies were willing to talk across the state lines - which would be a miracle in itself - they were not always involved in the day-to-day operations of the residential facilities. In Illinois, DCFS does not provide daily support to children removed from homes by the state. Instead, children are assigned to private care agencies responsible for the case management and most other services required by a child. Some, like Longwood, run group homes, residential facilities, and residential schools. DCFS only oversees the process. The system is similar to the America's private prison industry.

Many private agencies have good intentions and sincerely want to help the child under their care. However, for most, the priority is to have all of their beds filled. It is a matter of survival. Empty beds mean loss of revenue, which is a private agency's lifeline. At Longwood, the people in charge had nothing against Maurice, some even liked him, but sending Maurice home to Louisiana was the last thing on their minds. In order to keep him in the facility, official reports would say that Maurice was psychologically damaged, in need of treatment, and therefore not ready to relocate back to his home state. As Maurice was spending additional months locked behind dark walls and sinking deeper into the gloom of Longwood, his psychological damage was growing and he needed even more intensive treatment. No matter what, Maurice could not win.

Then, one day, Maurice ran away. He managed to sneak out unnoticed by security, and made it to downtown Chicago, where he took a bus and went home to New Orleans.

When Maurice showed up at his grandmother's doorstep, she was not impressed. "You did what?! You escaped like some convict? This is not how we do things in this family! We must contact the proper authorities immediately! I will explain that you are now home with me and that I am perfectly capable of taking care of you."

Unfortunately, the proper authorities could not care less about what grandma was or was not capable of. They grabbed Maurice and put him on the first bus back to Illinois. He was expected to continue with his treatment resulting from anxiety, which was a direct consequence of being separated from his family. The following day, Maurice was back at Longwood, sitting by the wall and wrapped in his dark blanket.

A few weeks later, Maurice escaped again. This time grandma did not notify the proper authorities. In a brief communication with a handful of people in Illinois whom he could trust, Maurice assured them that he was safe, and could not be happier. To hell with treatment – he had already forgotten about his anxiety and was not sad anymore. Maurice had plans to live on the bayous and work on his uncle's shrimping boat.

Who knows, maybe Maurice is still there today, swaying from the mast and arguing with God about not stopping Katrina and allowing for places like Longwood to exist.

CHAPTER TWO

Young and Deadly

The majority of boys residing at Longwood were not trying to be nice, sweet, or polite. They were tough. Despite their young age, they have seen and experienced things that damaged them for life. On one of those unseasonably warm spring days in northern Illinois, a van carrying a bunch of boys from Longwood drove by a wealthy suburban high school at the same time when students were being released. Many suburban boys wore sagging pants with their butts hanging out in a carefully cultivated *I am bad, and I am a gangbanger* look. "Why are those sorry mother....ers trying so hard to be like us? Do they think it's cool?" said Jamar to no one in particular. Jamar was a lifelong client of the child welfare system. *Don't they know that I would do anything to be like them? To have that life?* But Jamar would not dare to say that aloud.

At Longwood, everybody was always on guard, especially around strangers. At the same time, everyone was genuine and sincere - there was no pretending. You always knew who you were dealing with. Some of the boys were hardened criminals and some were murderers, or in the process of becoming one.

Most people, staff and residents alike, stayed away from Jose. When he was only fourteen, Jose attacked a seventy-two-year-old woman in the garage of her own house. Jose raped and tried to kill her, but the woman survived. Jose was caught and arrested. He went to trial, spent a long time in juvie, and eventually ended up at Longwood.

Jose heard voices. Maybe his voices told him to do crazy things, but nobody knew for sure, because the conversations between Jose and his voices were confidential. From time to time, it was possible to have a rational conversation with Jose, but the next minute, and always out of the blue, he would do something bizarre, like jumping out of the window of his therapist's office. The office was located on the first floor, no more than three feet above ground, but Jose jumped through a closed window and took the frame, screen, and glass with him. Another time, while at school, Jose removed a cover from the heating and cooling vent and started eating the trash that accumulated inside, from time to time taking a bite of his own arm. Jose had metal plates in his head from banging it against the walls. He attacked the school's principal with a sharpened pencil and only missed the principal's eye by half an inch.

Everyone thought that Jose belonged in a secure psychiatric ward and that, unless there was a major medical breakthrough, he should probably stay there for the rest of his life. Only no mental hospital was available or willing to take Jose, and so he stayed at Longwood where nobody knew how to deal with him or how to prevent his self-mutilation and his attacks. Everyone just hoped not to be near him when it happened.

Nobody, however, expected anything super crazy from D'Andre. D'Andre talked back to adults, developed a language in which profanities served as all parts of speech, fought other boys on daily basis, worked hard to jeopardize his treatment, failed at school, and ignored every single request, advice, or directive coming his way. In other words, at Longwood D'Andre acted like most other residents. It was only after leaving Longwood that D'Andre made the news. Following an argument with his girlfriend and the mother of his child, D'Andre killed his girlfriend's sister, father, and grandmother, and seriously injured her mother as well. Since Illinois put a moratorium on the death penalty, D'Andre is currently serving three consecutive life sentences plus sixty years[4].

People who knew D'Andre at Longwood said that nothing could have been done to prevent the tragedy, and nothing can be done to stop other residents from committing crimes after they are discharged and become too old for the system. Because of limited resources, limited staff, and limited everything else, treatment at Longwood was like putting a Band-Aid on a bullet hole.

Longwood residents were not natural born killers. They were all psychologically damaged, but this did not mean that they were all bad or that all of them were capable of harming people. For example, it would be hard to imagine someone more different from a stereotypical gangbanger and a juvenile criminal than Kwan.

Kwan was quiet and composed, intelligent, and soft-spoken. He was slim, fit, and moved with the agility of a feline. With his twin sister and older brother, Kwan grew up in a traditional two-parent household on a quiet and moderately affluent suburb of Chicago. His older brother went to medical school, but Kwan was more of an artist. He loved anime and showed promise at sketching and drawing. However, Kwan's father did not approve. Kwan was expected to earn good grades in all academic subjects and then select a respectful career, maybe follow in his brother's footsteps. What could go wrong in a nice family like that? How could someone like Kwan end up in a residential facility housing young criminals?

Kwan's family had a dark secret. Kwan's father was abusing his wife. Ever since Kwan could remember, his mother was beaten, yelled at, and humiliated. His mom never fought back. She applied make-up to cover cuts and bruises and told the kids that dad was just stressed out because he worked too hard, or that he was strict because of his upbringing. She told them that he provided for the entire family and deserved their respect, that it was really her fault. She said it did not hurt that much.

One evening, Kwan and his sister, Sunny, came home late from an event at school. The dad was in the process of dragging the mom by her hair, she was on the floor with her nose bleeding, and one eye was swollen shut. Kwan calmly went to the kitchen, grabbed a knife, and cut his father's throat.

CHAPTER THREE

Josh

Josh was the oldest of three siblings growing up in one of those struggling to survive small towns in Arkansas. The family was poor but so were most of their neighbors. To Josh, this was normal. Both parents worked, made a buck or two above the minimum wage, and nobody was starved. Life in rural Arkansas was cheap. Josh would tell you that his childhood was happy. He ended up at Longwood because of a bizarre chain of events.

One day, when Josh was eleven, his dad had a buddy spend a night in their house. Did Josh's father know that his buddy was a wanted fugitive? He probably knew but chose not to care, and not to share that information with his wife either. Josh's mom, busy with Josh and two younger siblings, and used to her husband's buddies coming and going all the time, could not care less who was drinking beer in her barn on that particular evening. This was a mistake that she would regret for the rest of her life.

In the middle of a night, when all three kids were fast asleep, a SWAT team in full combat gear stormed into the house and broke doors, windows, and several things in-between. The little ones started screaming. Josh just watched in frozen horror as mom and dad were thrown to the floor, handcuffed, and dragged outside. Both went to jail for aiding and abetting. The fact that mom had no idea that she was harboring a fugitive did not matter— according to law, you are supposed to know who is sleeping under your roof. Josh and his little siblings were collected by Child Protective Services.

It was never clear how Josh ended up in Illinois, where he seemingly had no relatives or ties. Supposedly, it was some obscure medical diagnosis that required special treatment available only in Chicago. The diagnoses later proved to be incorrect but the paperwork was done, and Josh stayed in the land of Lincoln.

A good-looking white boy with decent grades and an easy smile is much easier to place in a foster home than an African-American gangbanger who gave up on school after two weeks of kindergarten. Josh was lucky to end up in a rare foster home where the family actually cared. He moved to a big house in a beautiful suburb.

Josh continued to do well in school. He finished the eighth-grade and went on to a prestigious high school. The coaches soon discovered that Josh was a talented athlete and played football like there was no tomorrow. Josh soon joined the team and it seemed as though his future was bright.

In the very first game of the season, Josh's team obliterated their opponents. After the game, some other boys arranged a little celebration and introduced Josh to booze. In less than an hour, Josh was drunk as a skunk. In his drunken stupor, he had the brilliant idea of taking off all of his clothes and going for a triumphant run outside the locker room while being enthusiastically cheered by his equally drunk teammates. The school cop got involved, Child Protective Services was notified, and Josh was arrested for indecent exposure. Under Illinois laws, Josh was now considered a sex offender and possibly a subject to the sex offender registration for the rest of his life. As such, he was placed at Longwood.

Sex offenders do not evoke public sympathy. They are considered monsters. Public opinion would forgive a murderer but never a sex offender. In general, when people hear the words "sex offender," mothers grab the kids and run while fathers turn into superheroes and start loading their Smith & Wessons. People associate sex offenders with repulsive predators who prey on angelic little kids and rape the neighborhood virgins.

Contrary to this belief, sexual offenses actually represent a multitude of actions. Most of them, regardless of severity, may stigmatize the perpetrators for the rest of their lives. In a controversial case in Illinois, a sixteen-year-old honor roll student committed suicide after he was accused of child pornography. He allegedly played to his friends an audio recording of him and a girl while they had sex[5]. Under current laws, two sixteen-year-olds engaged in a consensual relationship can be charged with abusing each other. They can both end up on a sex offender list.

Josh was not even involved in anything sexual, but he indecently exposed himself in public, and that was enough to give him the label of sex offender, lock him at Longwood, and throw away the key. Some say that on that eventful night, he was not the only drunk teenage moron running around with a naked butt after a football game and that, in fact, he was joined by two other boys. But there was a significant difference between Josh and the other two: they had wealthy biological parents who immediately barricaded themselves behind an army of lawyers, while Josh was a youth in the care of the state.

Eventually, a juvenile judge decided that there was no sexual gratification attached to Josh's bare-butt victory run and, therefore, his act was a misdemeanor and not a felony. But the wheels of justice grind slowly and by the time this decision was rendered, it was too late for Josh to go back to his nice foster home. He remained at Longwood as another boy with nowhere to go.

Josh became depressed. His old dreams about being drafted by the NFL were replaced by new dreams about being able to walk down the street without supervision. He thought his future was over. All he wanted was to be with the people he loved. Josh had not seen his family for years, and he became obsessed with going home. He stopped caring about school and about grades. He stopped caring about his personal hygiene or about the clothes he wore, and he lost a significant amount of weight. Even getting him out of bed was a challenge.

Ironically, at the time of Josh's conviction, his mom back in Arkansas was free and gainfully employed. Even his dad was home on parole and working odd jobs. They got their two little ones back and were fervently fighting to be reunited with Josh. They were told that Josh could not be discharged because he was depressed and must continue with treatment. However, Josh was only depressed and in need of treatment because he could not be reunited with his mom and dad. Like Maurice and many other boys before him, Josh became entangled in a classic catch-22, child welfare edition. And like Maurice, one day Josh just disappeared. Acting in defiance of his extensive treatment plan, he ran away from Longwood and went home to Arkansas.

His mom cried when she was able to hold him again. Even the dad was emotional. At that moment, Josh's depression was miraculously cured.

Eventually, Josh finished high school and went to college. He had a girlfriend. He was happy again. The only difference between him and his college roommates was that Josh would never touch booze. For some reason, he hated the stuff.

CHAPTER FOUR

Angels from the Gridiron and Manicured Monsters

A person who works directly with wards of the state in a group home is called a residential counselor or a youth care worker. This person is grossly overworked and shamefully underpaid. At any given moment, a residential counselor may get injured, infected with something nasty, get arrested, or die. To be a residential counselor, one must have a clean criminal record and a high school diploma, however, employers prefer a college degree. The pay is about half of the national average, and the turnover rate is three times higher than the turnover rate for all other employees in the United States, comparable only to the fast-food industry.

After you are hired as a residential counselor, you have to go through physical restraints training, in which you are taught how to safely subdue a kid.

Nobody likes restraining kids, but sometimes it has to be done. When Jose was biting his own arm or banging his head against the walls, he had to be restrained. When several boys from rival street gangs managed to pick up rocks in the woods and started a fight with the sincere intention of killing one another, they had to be restrained. When sweet and quiet but also big and inhumanly strong Juan lost his temper, grabbed a porcelain cover of a toilet tank, and went after a boy who teased him, Juan had to be restrained. In that particular incident, Juan and the four grown men who tried to stop him all sustained various degrees of injuries.

Physical restraints are supposed to be safe and used only to prevent a minor from hurting himself or others. In reality, however, there is no such thing as a safe restraint. Sometimes things go terribly wrong and a horrible accident occurs, like the death of the very child that was supposed to be restrained.

In a 2016 incident at Allendale, another residential youth home in Illinois, sixteen-year-old Shaquan Allen died of asphyxiation during a restraint[6]. Shaquan had been there for over two years. About a year before his death, he was cleared to leave Allendale for a desirably less-restrictive setting. Unfortunately, less restrictive facilities are routinely overcrowded, and there was no bed available for Shaquan. Being promised relative freedom and then having this promise taken away is one of the primary reasons why wards of the states go into crisis and start smashing everything and everyone within their reach. Shaquan grew increasingly frustrated. One day, he lost his temper, snapped, had to be restrained, and died.

Two residential counselors were arrested and charged with obstruction of justice. One was also charged with involuntary manslaughter. Obstruction charges against the other man were later dropped. A twenty-four-page report was written, and DCFS announced that they would look into the problem of kids staying in residential facilities beyond their discharge dates. Cameras were installed all over Allendale.

The case was reported by the Chicago Tribune and other news organizations. The general public was provided with a rare glance into the residential youth care system, usually well hidden behind a thick veil of confidentiality and juvenile privacy laws. Media access into these facilities only occurs after some sort of death or tragic accident, and although this access is very short lived, it nevertheless succeeds in shocking the public with its findings.

The risk of dying applies to residents and staff alike. There was some media coverage about an incident involving a middle-aged female counselor in another facility. She was hit by a car while chasing after a teenage girl who tried to run away[7]. The woman was killed, and another residential counselor was injured.

Residential youth homes are chronically understaffed. Since kids must be watched and the required staff-to-residents' ratio must be maintained, employees are frequently asked to work overtime. People work sixty or sometimes even eighty-hour weeks, they are exhausted and overworked, and this is when bad things happen.

An additional risk to staff comes from infectious diseases. For several months, Longwood had a resident who was HIV positive. Typically, this information is confidential, but at Longwood, nothing remained secret for long. From time to time, institutions such as public-school districts have children who test positive for HIV, and it is not considered the end of the world. Laws do not require this information to be shared with anyone who works at the school. However, Longwood was different. Boys fought almost every day, and when they fought blood was everywhere and staff members were routinely exposed. In this particular case, the staff at Longwood became uncomfortable and asked how to handle the issue. They were given a box of latex gloves and told to carry on. After fights, residential counselors, teachers, and other school staff were required to clean up the HIV positive blood. There were no precautions and no training on how to do so safely.

Like all group homes for wards of the states, staff at Longwood had its share of angels and demons. The angels looked nothing like cherubs from the Renaissance paintings. Sometimes, they were ex-military. There was always a handful who retired from professional or semi-professional sports. There was Mr. G who used to play for the Chicago Bears, Mr. R who was in the NCAA and then played semi-professionally in Wisconsin, and Mr. A., who was a professional boxer. They worked at Longwood not because they had to but because it was a choice that they made. They were giving back to the community. Many of them came from poor inner-city neighborhoods, and they never forgot what that life was like.

They were patient and disciplined. They elicited enormous respect, and when they spoke, the boys listened. They did not have to yell. They never used excessive force with a kid. They were always willing to come early and stay after hours to play basketball with the boys or to take them for a run. After the Chicago Bulls Organization donated brand new hoops, sports at Longwood, supervised by the professional athletes, became a serious affair.

There was also the fantastic Mr. Bob, a maintenance extraordinaire. Mr. Bob somehow kept the crumbling buildings at Longwood from falling apart, made sure that a mile-long road through the woods was accessible, and always walked around with his big toolbox fixing broken windows and holes in the walls punched by the boys. He even took several boys who showed interest under his wing and taught them how to use basic tools, how to build a bench, and how to make simple repairs. Unknowingly to himself, Mr. Bob was running the only vocational program available at Longwood until the management found out and ordered him to stop. The boys were not supposed to learn how to use a drill or a hammer because it was not in their treatment plans. The boys were only supposed to contemplate life and ponder the question of existence in anticipation of their next therapy session.

There were also those among staff who preyed on the kids. Sometimes, you could see people carrying big bags from the back of the kitchen to their cars. One person bragged that she was always claiming at least five residents as dependents on her tax returns. From time to time, a new counselor seemed to enjoy restraining kids a little bit too much. However, the sexual predators were by far the worst.

Mrs. Jasmine was an attractive married woman in her early thirties. A male counselor walked in on her when she was engaged in sexual intercourse with a sixteen-year-old boy. At least three other boys said that they had similar encounters with Mrs. Jasmine and that she was always inviting and ready. In order to avoid a scandal, the management asked Mrs. Jasmine to quietly resign. Mrs. Jasmine was hired by another residential facility less than a year later and, because she had prior experience, was given a management position.

Miss Guadalupe was short, on the fat side, and forty-seven years old, but this did not stop her from engaging in a sexual relationship with Jamar, who was only seventeen. The following year, after he turned eighteen, Miss Guadalupe invited Jamar to move in with her. She never tried to hide the fact that they were a couple. She believed that she was doing Jamar a favor, but Jamar did not share her enthusiasm. He would tell others that he could no longer look at himself in the mirror and that he wished he was never born. But after being discharged from Longwood, Jamar had nowhere to go.

Even though the prevailing attitude at Longwood was to pretend that the sexual exploitation of minors did not occur, its existence was all but an inarguable fact known to everyone. Reporting to management was pointless because they wanted proof, and witnessing an incident or hearing about it from the boys was not considered reliable. When confronted, people involved would deny everything. Management did not want to be investigated, and especially did not want to deal with the aftermath. A young boy was coerced into having sex with someone three times his age? So what? Life must go on, and there is always therapy available to the kid. We can also arrange a prescription for more meds.

CHAPTER FIVE

Stick Shift

Those boys who managed to run away from Longwood and went home to Louisiana or Arkansas would not have been able to do it without help. Someone had to take care of the logistics, tell the kids what to do, and give them money for the train or bus. Assisting not just a minor but a minor youth-in-care in crossing state lines is illegal. The staff members who did this took a significant risk. These people had to make a difficult moral decision and take action when the agency would not because the agency was too greedy to let a kid like Maurice or Josh go home.

This does not mean, however, that other boys at Longwood were not trying to escape by themselves, without assistance, and having no idea what was involved. These kids were rarely successful, and most were either brought back or returned on their own.

One day, when residential counselors attended a big staff meeting, three boys decided to make a run for it. They broke into the staff locker room, took a set of keys, and stole a counselor's car. Out of more than fifty vehicles in the parking lot that day, they had to steal the only one with a manual transmission. What happened next was a spectacular event, worthy of a movie script. Demond, the boy behind the wheel, had maybe two hours of driving experience in his entire life, all of it unsupervised. He somehow put the stolen car in first gear and managed to move it, but that was all Demond knew how to do. Demond either did not know that there was more than one gear, or knew but had no clue how to switch a gear while disengaging the clutch. Nevertheless, Demond was trying to drive fast in first gear. Eventually, four squad cars, representing the entire local police force, were called to the scene and followed with screaming sirens and flashing lights, while the engine of the stolen car wailed in loud protest.

The car finally gave up; the engine blew and produced enough fumes to create a dramatic smoke screen. And then, Demond slowly emerged from the smoke with his hands up and his two sidekicks close behind. It put an end to fun and games for that day, and everyone was told to go home. Only the owner of the car was not amused, as he was left to pay for the repairs.

When a resident tried to run away on foot, staff was required to follow. Usually, it was a bizarre, slow-motion event. A resident would walk, and several staff members walked a few steps behind him not trying to physically stop the boy. Putting hands on a resident who did not pose a danger to himself or others would not be justified and therefore was not allowed. So, the group just walked. If the boy stopped, others stopped as well. If he started running, others would increase their speed to a trot. Whenever the residents were bored, they enjoyed engaging staff members in this game, providing residential counselors, therapists, and teachers with regular exercise.

Not far from the facility, the group would pass the Pond of a Thousand Shoes. It was not really a pond, but a swamp where generations of residential counselors and other employees lost at least one shoe, stuck in the mud while following a kid. But with shoes or without them, the slow-motion chase would continue until the resident reached and crossed certain points marking the boundaries of the property. When this happened, staff was allowed to call the cops, who would take over the chase. The boys knew this and, not wanting to deal with the police, usually arranged running activities just from one property marker to another.

On rare occasions, when there was more than one crisis taking place at the same time, the boys would leave unnoticed. It happened with two African-American inner-city kids, Jamir and DeAnthony, who were just brought to Longwood from Chicago. The boys never saw a real cornfield, and they never encountered dangerous wildlife like a cow. Nevertheless, they decided to run away from Longwood, which required walking across several miles of relatively dense woods. Jamir later said that they were hopelessly lost after less than five minutes. For hours, they fought the thick vegetation of the Illinois jungle, probably walking in circles, until finally they made it out of the woods and entered a nearby village. There, they decided to hitchhike. Little did they know that they placed themselves in the middle of a one-hundred percent white, Trump supporting, NRA loving, hunting, and beer drinking conservative stronghold. When people in that area see a black kid wearing sagging pants, they do not stop their trucks to offer assistance. They roll up the windows and step on the gas.

After several hours of trying to hitch a ride, Jamir and DeAnthony felt defeated and ready to faint from exhaustion. They threw themselves in front of a passing police car and announced to a surprised officer, "We ran away from Longwood. Just take us back!"

CHAPTER SIX

¡Yo Amo México!

Pablo did not want to leave Mexico. In fact, he hated the idea. At eleven, he wanted to stay with his friends and play soccer, which to him was the purpose of his existence and the greatest love of his life. However, Pablo's family had plans of their own and, one day, he was smuggled across the border together with mom, dad, and three little siblings. Due to another strange twist of fate and a major family disaster, four years later Pablo ended up at Longwood.

Pablo was brilliant. By the time he arrived at Longwood, he already spoke English like a native, he was a straight-A student and devoured knowledge. He also excelled in sports. When he was not on a soccer field or a basketball court, he would be doing homework or reading a book. He did not get involved in fights, nor did he condone violence at all. Pablo was a natural leader, and other boys looked up to him. He was always treating people with respect and evoked respect from others. He was one of those rare individuals consistently in full control of their temper and never raised his voice. Pablo was tirelessly positive, and wore a Mona Lisa smile on his intelligent face. Pablo even dressed differently. He was leaner and taller than most other boys and preferred polo shirts and dark jeans that fit around his waist, instead of sagging to the floor. The only unique thing about Pablo's appearance was a large pendant with the Virgin Mary hanging around his neck. To Pablo, this had a special meaning.

Pablo started the famous Longwood Math Club. At some point, Longwood hired a special education teacher who actually knew high school math and was able to teach it. While a handful of boys – the ones who were genuinely interested in learning a thing or two at school - could keep up with other subjects, it was challenging to learn advanced math on their own. So, Pablo had a chat with the teacher, "There are four of us who want to learn high school math. We want to learn it all. Can you teach us?"

No teacher can deny such a request. Mr. G., the one who retired from the Chicago Bears, offered help as an assistant and for many months, the Math Club was meeting every day before school, after school, and at lunch. Its four members were getting tons of homework and kept asking for more. Even the perpetually greedy management was impressed to the point of opening their wallet and buying several graphing calculators.

In just a few months, the club members completed a year of algebra. It was followed by an intensive course of high school geometry. Then, the club moved on to advanced algebra and trigonometry and even touched calculus. Pablo was always in the lead.

If you visited Longwood during that time, you would see a bunch of napping boys, bored with life in general. A couple would be staring blankly at the walls. Some would play a game, rap, maybe fight or entertain themselves by having a loud argument. But then, you would see something strange. One boy, unusually tall for a Hispanic, would be fervently scribbling something in a notebook. A residential counselor would approach him and say,

"Hey, what up, Pablo? Whaddya doing?"

"Nothin' much, Mr. B. Just rationalizing denominators in radical expressions."

Pablo was an illegal immigrant. His therapists were telling him that DCFS was going to give him a Green Card, and that a juvenile court judge would make him a permanent resident of the United States. The math teacher kept saying that Pablo should not listen and that neither DCFS nor a circuit court judge was even remotely qualified to decide on an immigration case. The math teacher kept saying that it falls outside of their jurisdiction and that only the federal government could do it, but Pablo did not care. Yes, having a Green Card would be nice, but he never intended to come to the United States anyway, and he was not going to stay here. He wanted to go back to Mexico, the homeland that he loved and missed. He even had a plan: at first, he would live with his grandma in Mexico, where he would start to make a life for himself. He would continue with his education and he would play some serious soccer again. He would be home. Home! Why, on Earth, would anyone assume that he wanted to stay in the United States? Pablo was Mexican and proud of it.

Then Pablo turned eighteen. He finished high school with the highest honors. He was finally ready and eager to go home to Mexico. Unfortunately, the management at Longwood prohibited Pablo from leaving. They said that he had to stay and continue with his treatment. His bed had to remain filled.

The math teacher was enraged and told Pablo that he should get up, walk out of the door, turn south, and keep walking until he reaches Mexico. But Pablo would not rock the boat. If they did not want him to leave yet, he would stay, at least for now. Apparently, they had to have a good reason to keep him there.

Pablo stayed at Longwood doing absolutely nothing. There was nothing for him to do besides occasional sports or chess games. The residents who graduated from high school would go to a half-empty room above their old classrooms and watch TV or sleep. Their days were filled with boredom. From time to time, they would see a therapist and complain about life being empty and meaningless and about not having options for the future. But their beds were filled, and the flow of money to Longwood was secure.

Pablo was a foreign national, over eighteen-years-old, who did not commit a crime in the United States, and who expressed a clear intention to return to his native country. He was locked in a residential facility in the US and kept there against his will. It would be hard to say how many international laws were broken, but nobody cared. In the land of rapidly growing xenophobia and the most profound contempt for illegal immigrants, Pablo was forced to continue living in a country that claimed to not want him in the first place, even though he wanted nothing more than to leave.

After a while, Pablo was finally discharged from Longwood but still not allowed to go home to Mexico. Department of Children and Family Services placed him in a Transitional Living Program in Rockford, Illinois. The therapists told Pablo not to worry because his life is going to improve – he will get a

Driver's License, and they will send him to college.

Unfortunately, getting a Driver's License was impossible because Pablo was an illegal immigrant. Going to college was also impossible for the same reason. Pablo would love to get a job, but as illegal, he could not be hired. Pablo did not want this life and he kept asking to let him return to Mexico, but it was still not allowed. He had to continue with treatment, and to achieve this ambitious goal, he was required to remain in a shabby apartment that was arranged for him and several other boys, and to see a therapist once a week, which required a two-and-a-half hour walk each way. Even Pablo was slowly losing hope. His old math teacher was screaming on the phone, "Screw them all, Pablo! You are a free man! Just pack your things, or don't pack them, and go!"

Eventually, despite his therapist and case manager ordering him to stay, Pablo went home. He was scared and genuinely uncomfortable with this decision. He felt like he was doing something wrong. The trip was made in secret, far away from the prying eyes of DCFS. It was the first documented case of an illegal immigrant being smuggled to Mexico from the United States.

Today, Pablo lives in Ciudad Juárez in Mexico, not far from El Paso, Texas. In 2018, he earned a college degree in industrial engineering. He plays soccer. He is also working for a large electronics company and has recently bought a house. In 2019 Pablo married a beautiful young woman, and his old math teacher attended their wedding. Pablo said that he never regretted his decision to leave the United States. Life is good, and the future looks bright.

CHAPTER SEVEN

Of Love, Bolts, and Monopoly Games

The boys who were placed at Longwood had limited contact with the outside world. Other than medical appointments or mandatory court appearances, they almost never left the facilities, except on the rare occasions when they were allowed to go home. Just a few boys were able to earn that privilege, and not all of them had families to go to. Even for those who did, home visits were few and far between. The residents were also not allowed to have cell phones or to use cell phones that belonged to staff.

The residents had almost no interactions with other kids their age. They did not attend a regular school, nor did they participate in community events. In fact, the community was trying very hard to pretend that Longwood did not exist. Local law enforcement had nightmares about Longwood and its occupants. Sometimes, cops were called to Longwood three times on the same day. Other than home visits available just to a few, boys would leave only when they were allowed to go shopping, usually at Walmart, and always closely supervised.

Some boys stayed at Longwood for years. Being cut off from the outside world, they had few opportunities to develop appropriate social skills. Ironically, most of the boys had already managed to father children of their own. They had feelings for their kids and wanted to see them from time to time but not one ever expressed a desire to marry the mother of his child and not one planned to be permanently present in his child's life. When asked about child support, they laughed.

On top of everything else that was wrong with their lives, the boys had to deal with raging hormones. Only one boy was openly homosexual, while most were sexual opportunists and experimented with sexual activities with one another simply because they had no access to anything else.

At Longwood, violence was a permanent feature of daily life. Fights were frequent and everyone was inured to them. Only sometimes, and only when things got really serious, the perpetrator would be taken to a juvenile detention center or jail. Usually, he would come back after a day or two because the juvie and jails were permanently overcrowded and would not keep boys who already stayed in a restricted facility.

Every single boy was in therapy. Almost all therapists were young, white females with limited or no experience, dedicated but not equipped to work with this demographic. The boys enjoyed therapy and frequently discussed it among themselves. When this happened, the main topic of conversation was usually the therapists' boobs or butt. Older and more experienced therapists would not accept employment for the pathetic salary offered by a residential facility housing wards of the state.

Almost all boys were heavily medicated. Since the facility was chronically understaffed and some boys could not be handled, turning them into zombies was considered a feasible solution. Most boys would admit that they were hopelessly addicted to the medication they were prescribed.

With few exceptions, the boys were constantly depressed or at least under an excessive amount of stress. They had childhood memories that kept giving them nightmares, and they did not want to think about their future. They were old enough and realistic enough to believe that the future they did have was bleak at best. They were not provided with many opportunities to develop useful skills. Even though they acquired some theoretical knowledge at the residential school, *theoretical* was not what they needed. There was no vocational training available to them.

Although it may sound like a paradox, the boys were street-smart, but they did not really know how to function in the outside world. They knew how to survive a night in a gang-infested *hood*, but they did not know how to replace a light bulb. On top of that, they were heavily addicted to the psychotropic drugs that were given to them at Longwood, but they knew that after they age out of the system, the prescriptions would stop. They were going to need something to replace the meds. Meth? Booze?

Some boys developed elaborate plans to commit a crime immediately after being discharged with the sole purpose of returning to prison as soon as possible. They told stories about their predecessors who did it. You steal something, break a few things in the process, maybe assault a person or two, and you will be safe in a prison where you will have a roof over your head and regular meals. You will even get your meds. After all, being institutionalized was something they knew; this was something they were experts in.

Sometimes, a boy would start screaming and was unable to stop. Other times, a boy would hurt himself or try to end his life. When things got serious, a resident would be SASSed and taken to a hospital. SASS, which stands for Screening, Assessment and Support Services, is a program developed in Illinois to provide assistance to children and adolescents who experience a mental health crisis. A boy in crisis was usually taken from Longwood to Riverside, a behavioral healthcare center which, for all practical purposes, was a mental hospital. A boy would stay there for a few weeks, get even more meds, get better, come back, get depressed again, try to hurt himself, get SASSed, go to Riverside, stay for a couple of weeks, and so on. Unless the boy aged out of the system, the cycle had no end.

Riverside was also an unusual setting for a famous love story involving a boy, a girl, and some metal objects. The hero of the story was Eddie, a white sixteen-year-old Longwood resident. Eddie was an intelligent and good-looking kid, but after being brought to Longwood, he quickly lost interest in life. He stopped paying attention in classes, neglected his personal hygiene, and some mornings he would not even get dressed and came to school wearing slippers and pajamas. One day, Eddie lost the last glimmer of hope and tried to commit suicide. After failing, he was taken to Riverside.

At Riverside, Eddie met a girl who also attempted suicide. They had a lot in common. They provided each other with emotional support. They fell in love and, in turn, found a new reason to live.

This love story was brutally interrupted when Eddie was sent back to Longwood — he could not leave the love of his life behind! He had to go back to Riverside, and he had to do it fast because his Juliet was waiting in tears! In the name of love, Eddie was ready to do whatever it took. After giving it thorough consideration, Eddie developed a plan: he went to Longwood's dark recreational room and swallowed a handful of metal pieces from a Monopoly game. He did not eat them all, but he swallowed enough to be taken back to the hospital and reunited with the lady who stole his heart.

Unfortunately, after only one week, Eddie was discharged again. His return to Longwood was not exactly happy because, not only did it break his heart all over again, but now Eddie was also hated by all other boys for ruining their Monopoly setup. Eddie, however, could not care less because his heart, his mind, and his soul were busy longing for a certain young lady locked in a tower in Riverside.

All the staff members were aware of Eddie's infliction and stayed diligent. Everything that was made of metal, glass, wood, plastic, or stone, and everything that was even remotely poisonous or dangerous, was taken away from Eddie's room, but the naïve personnel underestimated the power of love. Eddie somehow managed to remove the screws from a toilet tank and swallowed them in one gulp. He was retaken to Riverside.

The incident was a source of interesting dialogues among the boys. "What do you think?" asked Tavon. "Is he going to beep every time he walks through the security gate in court? Are the cops going to see Monopoly pieces on the screen?"

Even quiet and inhumanely strong Juan had something to say, "Pussy! A real man in love would not swallow screws but bolts…"

CHAPTER EIGHT

Born Male, Poor, and Black

Most cultural anthropologists say that humans have no instincts. Although the great debate about nature vs. nurture continues, scientists generally agree that other than reflexes – such as yawning, blinking, or sneezing – human behaviors have to be learned. The American eel knows that in order to breed it must make a journey of over fifteen-hundred miles from Nova Scotia to the Sargasso Sea in the Atlantic. A robin does not have to be taught how to build a nest, nor does a spider need to attend school to learn how to thread a web.

Humans are not born knowing. Humans must learn. We may have genetic predispositions, such as when someone says, "She is such a great singer. It runs in her family." However, without learning, we would not be able to survive. It starts when we are babies and continues throughout our lives. This is why our childhood experiences are relevant, and this is why having responsible parents is crucial to our development. This is why responsible parents make such a fuss about sending their children to a good school, or demand that they do their homework and receive good grades.

Maslow, who was an American psychologist, helped to explain these human behaviors by developing a hierarchy of needs. He created a pyramid, which is still widely accepted by modern psychologists, where he placed basic needs at the bottom and more sophisticated ones on top. He said that people must have their lower needs satisfied before they can move on to the next level. If you are starving or if you are outside exposed to the elements in a blizzard, you would not care about listening to Chopin's Prelude in e minor. You would just want to eat and get warm. After being clothed and fed, you would then desire shelter; somewhere you could feel protected and safe. Then, after all of this, you would want to belong. Humans are social beings, and we therefore usually want to be a member of a family, a group, a community or a society. The next level is self-esteem. We want to give and receive love, we want freedom, and we want to be appreciated. Finally, when all of these needs are satisfied, we can move on to the highest level. After reaching the top of the pyramid, one might work towards a Ph.D., become a political leader, create a masterpiece, or listen to Chopin's prelude.

And now, think about the boys at Longwood in terms of nature vs. nurture, and in terms of the Maslow's hierarchy of needs. Even before they were born, they were already doomed. Their pregnant mothers drank alcohol, used drugs, or both. The boys were born with fetal alcohol syndrome or fetal drug syndrome. If they were lucky, they only developed ADD or ADHD and had poor reasoning skills. The less fortunate would have at least mild mental retardation and a slew of medical problems. The least lucky were born with severe deformities and a significant intellectual delay.

After they were abused by nature, it was time for nurture to play dirty tricks on them. When they were little, their most fundamental needs were not met. They did not have enough to eat. They may have had a shelter but it was dirty, neglected, and the utilities were probably cut off. In the winter, they were cold, and in the summer, they suffered from excessive heat.

Most boys never met their fathers, and they often had no idea who their fathers were. They had mothers who were not interested in teaching them anything. They were yelled at, beaten, and they never felt safe. These kids grew up thinking that this was just how things were. They learned that this was how the world worked. Their older siblings would beat their younger siblings and mom's current boyfriend would beat mom unless he was busy beating her kids. This was not considered abuse, but simply a way of life. If there was love or affection, it came as a rare commodity. In many cases, a grandmother was the only somewhat reliable and caring presence in their lives.

Their life skills were abysmal. For example, encouraged by teachers, a bunch of boys at Longwood wanted to build a pond and a garden behind the school, and they were given permission from management to do a little fundraiser among the staff. They offered a car wash but, unfortunately, none of the kids knew how to actually wash a car. They had never done it before, nor had they ever even seen it done.

The majority of boys who resided at Longwood were born and raised in the most dangerous Chicago neighborhoods. The city of Chicago has a vibrant culture, fascinating history, and genuinely fantastic architecture. It has a beautiful downtown and an alluring Gold Coast, excellent sports teams, lovely parks, and gorgeous beaches along Lake Michigan. It has the Magnificent Mile, the Willis Tower, the Navy Pier, the Arts Institute, the McCormick Place, and the Lake Shore Drive. Chicago is easy to love.

On the other hand, five hundred-seventy people were murdered in Chicago in 2018. Every two minutes and twenty-nine seconds, someone in the city was involved in a shooting. Every fifteen hours a person was killed. Crime can happen anywhere in Chicago, but it is usually taking place in one of the predominantly African American neighborhoods[8].

The number of homicides in Chicago in 2018 was higher than the number of homicides in Denmark, Ireland, Greece, Portugal, Switzerland, Finland, Iceland, Norway, Austria, Sweden, Czech Republic, and Slovakia combined. The total population of those twelve countries is over eighty-five million. The city of Chicago has less than three million residents.

Among those murdered in Chicago, three hundred fifty-six, or sixty-two percent, were African American, and twenty-nine percent were either Hispanic or could not be identified in terms of race. Few were white. The majority of victims were African American males between thirteen and thirty-four-year-old. In Chicago, if you are male, young, and black, you have a good chance of getting killed.

Other than violence, there were additional contributing factors that shaped the early lives of the boys at Longwood. Unemployment in Chicago was fifty percent higher than the national average, and the poverty level was forty-six percent higher as well. Unemployment and poverty beget despair, and despair begets violence and crime. In the beautiful city of Chicago people get killed, especially when they are poor, male, and black.

At Longwood, most boys had a relative who was killed or at least knew someone who was killed. They would state matter-of-factly that if they ever go back, they will probably die, and they did not mean of an old age. That belief intensified after LaMarcus went to his cousin's funeral. His cousin was one of those impoverished inner-city idealists who believed that hard work and perseverance were his ticket out. So, the cousin studied like there was no tomorrow. After graduating from high school, he was accepted by a four-year college out of town. He finished his first year, did well on final exams, came home for the summer and brought a friend. They were both gunned down when they were walking down the street. For them, there was no tomorrow. They both died at the scene.

At Longwood, the prevailing belief was that you could not escape your fate and that hope was a dangerous commodity. However, there were precious few who tried. After being discharged from Longwood, Cavonte, one of the members of Pablo's Math Club, went to a community college. He had no money, no support, he never saw the inside of a museum, and he never went to a concert, or a play. He had no computer and no TV. He had no car and no Driver's License because, at Longwood,

Driver's Education was taught only in theory. To get to his classes, he had to endure a commute by public transportation combined with several long walks.

Another believer was Thomas, also a member of the Math Club who had a lifelong dream of becoming a mortician. He used to say to his math teacher, "I appreciate everything you are doing for me and, thanks to you, I have a chance to go to college. But I hate handouts. One day, I will return the favor. After you die, I will take a good care of you, and that's a promise."

Even though Cavonte and Thomas still believed, most other boys stopped a long time ago.

CHAPTER NINE

Anything Can Be a Weapon

In the Land of Plenty, being a teenager is not easy. A recent cartoon popularized through social media shows an old man and a teenage boy comparing their school experience.

"In my school," says the old man, "we had to wear uniforms, we were punished for being disrespectful to teachers, and we had to follow a lot of rules."

"And in my school," responds the boy, "I had to hide in a closet while a mass shooter was killing my friends and teachers."

Once again, in the summer of 2019, one of the most popular back-to-school items on many parents' shopping list was a bulletproof backpack. In the United States, parents of school-age children are no longer worried about schools providing their kids with adequate instruction, proper nutrition, and a sufficient amount of physical exercise. Nowadays, they just want their kids to survive the school day, preferably in one piece. Between 2015 and 2019 ninety-eight American students were killed and more than two hundred were injured in school shootings, but 2019 is far from over.

In Lincoln Academy, which was part of the Longwood residential complex, and where residents went to school, students shooting other students was never a problem. Students had absolutely and categorically no access to firearms. It was a priority among all staff members to make sure that no guns were never smuggled to Longwood. Everyone knew that with this demographic of students, providing anyone with a gun would turn the entire place into a morgue in a matter of minutes.

This did not mean that students were not trying to kill one another whenever they had a chance. In places like Longwood, juvenile offenders are housed together with no regard for their gang affiliations, and this approach creates a deadly mix. At Longwood, the two largest groups of residents were African-Americans and Latinos, both mostly from Chicago. The first group represented the Folk Nation, while the second one belonged to the People Nation. Some black kids from the city - a.k.a. the Folk - were affiliated with Gangster Disciples, while some Hispanic kids - a.k.a. the People - were affiliated with the Latin Kings. Gangster Disciples and Latin Kings do not get along.

At a personal level, a black kid housed at Longwood might have nothing against a Latino kid in the adjacent room. However, these consistently and habitually undisciplined boys followed their Gang Members Procedural Manual to a T. And the Procedural Manual says that whenever you encounter a member of a rival gang, you are required to implement B.O.S. (Beating on Sight) or, preferably, T.O.S. (Terminating on Sight) procedures. Many residents had a sincere intention of terminating other residents, and staff members did everything humanly possible to prevent it.

The first step in averting a bloodbath was identifying members of specific gangs. After this was done, anything that might even hint at gang affiliation was strictly forbidden. For example, the boys were not allowed to wear hats because, and this is something that everyone at Longwood knew, turning your hat to the right meant that you were Folk, and turning it to the left indicated your alliance with People. The boys enjoyed drawing, scribbling, and adorning their bodies with makeshift tattoos. Residential counselors and teachers joined forces in discouraging any artwork displaying three- or five-point crowns or six-pointed stars. A crown is a symbol of the Latin Kings, while the star represents the Disciples.

Longwood never had problems with white supremacists, however. If one would ever show up, both Kings and Disciples would kill him with their bare hands on the spot.

Despite the staff's efforts, preventing gang symbols was basically pointless because everyone already knew who was affiliated with which gang. Therefore, staff members were continually making herculean efforts to ensure that residents did not have access to weapons. Unfortunately, all employees soon learned a simple truth: that almost anything can be turned into a weapon, and that the boys could demonstrate impressive creativity in turning innocent objects into something sinister and deadly.

Chairs and tables would be broken, and their parts would be used as clubs. If a boy could put his hands on a chain and wrap it around the club, the end result was even more deadly. It created something like Negan's *Lucille* in the popular T.V. series, *The Walking Dead*. For this reason, at Longwood chains were not allowed, but the boys soon replaced them with metal spirals meticulously removed from spiral notebooks. Consequently, spiral notebooks and textbooks were also banned.

Manual pencil sharpeners supplied the residents with razor blades. Attached to strings, they turned into dangerous whips. Pieces of metal removed from plastic scissors could be easily transformed into knives. All spray devices, like aerosol insect killers, combined with lighters, which were easy to steal at Walmart, turned into impressive flamethrowers. Many cleaning supplies served the same purpose. For a while, teachers at Lincoln Academy were perplexed by a sudden popularity of the White-Out Liquid Paper. They soon realized that students would put it on multiple layers of folded and glued paper, let it dry, and use as effective slingshot bullets with sharp edges. And the list goes on, even without including the obvious weapons of mass destruction like sharpened pencils.

Residential counselors were not fond of breaking up the fights, especially when willing participants were members of rival gangs, or when a fight would involve some kind of weapon. Counselors were still required to stop these fights and implement a safe restraint on the kids. All employees knew, however, that in places like Longwood, a safe restraint was an oxymoron. You were either safe by staying far away from the juvenile gangsters, or you stepped in, stopped the fight, and got injured in the process, and you prayed that you did not accidentally hurt one of the kids.

In winter, employees would painstakingly remove icicles hanging from the low roof of the school building. The boys probably did not know that this was a weapon of choice among the members of the Russian mafia who were in charge of whacking people—after the job the icicle would melt, leaving zero trace of a murder weapon. Longwood residents came to the same conclusion, and icicles were also popular among the boys. When there was absolutely nothing else available to cause harm, the boys would use rocks, stones, or even pebbles which they would pick outside and wrap into a piece of clothing. No matter what preventive measures were implemented by the personnel, the boys were always one step ahead.

CHAPTER TEN

LGBT

Most Longwood residents followed the philosophy of living in the moment and not thinking about the future because, to them, the future looked bleak. Yet, they were only teenagers, and from time to time, especially the younger ones allowed themselves to dream. Their dreams were usually the same and always unrealistic: they would dream of becoming a professional football or basketball player or a famous rapper, of making millions, living in a mansion, and driving an exotic car. They would dream about fame and fortune.

Demetrius was one of these dreamers who actually had genuine talent. If anyone at Longwood had a remote chance of achieving fame, it was Demetrius. Demetrius could draw, and his sketches were astonishing. Using just a pencil, Demetrius could produce your portrait with an impressive likeness, or he could create some imaginary world so unique and vivid and with such attention to detail that you wanted to be there. Demetrius had no formal training, but everyone agreed that he should get one. Some staff members even started a collection to buy him oil paints, brushes, and canvas, but management eventually found out and issued a memo disallowing the teachers to continue their collection.

Demetrius was a tall, good-looking African American boy with stunning almond-shaped eyes. He was always well dressed and had a hint of eccentricity to his style, at least, to the greatest extent possible within the confines of his meager resources allocated for clothing. From time to time, Longwood would receive donations of used clothes. While most boys considered them worthless, Demetrius could always find something that, after a few alterations, looked terrific on him.

Demetrius was a good conversationalist and an original thinker, always asking interesting questions and enjoying philosophical debates. Sometimes, however, this was his downfall because Demetrius could be stubborn as a mule. He did not like admitting that he was wrong, and when he had his mind set on something, he would refuse to see things from a different perspective. Demetrius was a king among drama queens and loved making a scene whenever and wherever he could.

Demetrius was also openly gay. While some may think that being locked in an all-male facility was a gay paradise, Demetrius would say that nothing was further from the truth. He had high standards, and he was one of the very few Longwood residents who understood the difference between sex and love. Demetrius wanted love, he wanted to find someone special who would accept him, and who would love him back. While Longwood was full of sexual opportunists who had sex with everyone and everything that was around them, Demetrius was the only homosexual. Surprisingly, other boys would leave him alone, and he was rarely teased or bullied because of his sexual orientation. While Demetrius would probably have a hard time in a typical high school, the unique environment of Longwood was more progressive and less homophobic. Residents were even more accepting of Demetrius than some employees.

Demetrius grew up in a conservative two-parent home in a Chicago neighborhood with a reputation of being desirable and safe. Demetrius was the youngest of three siblings, and his two older sisters were already married. His father was a serious, hard-working man, and as far back as Demetrius could remember, dad always had more than one job. Whenever his dad was home, he would do some repairs or improvements around the house. They owned what was called a Chicago two-flat. In the past, the top floor was rented to strangers, but after the oldest sister got married and had her first kid, she and her husband moved in upstairs. The mom never worked, but she was always busy. Their place was meticulously clean and well-organized. Demetrius believed that his mother was the best cook on Earth.

There was one more pivotal element to Demetrius' life story: his entire family was Jehovah's Witnesses.

Demetrius was always gay. He did an excellent job explaining his sexual preferences to others. He said that it was something he had always felt compelled to do, and that he was never interested in girls. He would also say that people cannot even imagine how it feels, that it would be like trying to describe a January blizzard in Chicago to someone from Equatorial Africa, without even showing him a picture. You do not choose to be gay; you just are. Nothing changed you, nobody influenced you, and you certainly did not want it any more than other people wanted to be straight. Some guys are short, some are tall, some are weak while others are strong, and some guys are gay. To a gay man, making out with a woman would be weird, gross, and repulsive.

Demetrius' first big crush happened in the summer before high school. His name was Martin, and he was older, already a freshman in college. Martin was white, he had blue eyes and hair the color of dried, sun-bleached grass. Always defiant of a brush, his hair went in all directions. Martin was a true artist, and his major was graphic design. They became friends, but Martin never allowed it to be anything more. Martin broke up with his then boyfriend and was not in a relationship, but he would say that Demetrius was way too young and that Martin was not a pedophile. He was always saying it with a smile, but he was not joking. Martin drew a line which he would not allow Demetrius to cross.

Demetrius and Martin had more in common than just art. Martin also grew up in a conservative, traditional family, although his parents were not Jehovah's Witnesses. They were devout Catholics who moved to the United States from Eastern Europe before Martin was born.

Near the end of his first semester in college, Martin decided to tell his parents that he was homosexual. When he did, his father completely lost it. Without even saying a word, he started beating Martin, first with his fists but then with whatever he could grab. His dad was a big guy who worked in construction, and he knew how to beat a person to a pulp. Maybe if Martin fought back, it would not have been so bad, but for some reason he did not.

Demetrius was not there when it happened, and knew only what he heard from others. At first, Martin screamed and pleaded with his father, but then, he became quiet. He eventually lost consciousness. The beating continued for another thirty minutes or so until neighbors finally pulled Martin's father away. By the end of it, Martin was barely recognizable as a human being.

Martin spent weeks in a hospital. He survived but sustained permanent brain damage. His dreams of becoming a graphic designer or earning a college degree were over. For the rest of his life, Martin will need assistance with such activities as eating, dressing up, or going to the bathroom. His father never went to jail. Immediately after turning his son into little more than a vegetable, he went back to his native country, probably with a sense of accomplishment and work well done. His son will never be gay again. His son will never be anything.

As a tribute to Martin, Demetrius decided to come out of the closet. One Saturday evening with his family, after they finished their daily prayers and a family meal, he announced that he was gay. He knew his parents were not going to be happy, but he had the glimmer of hope that maybe, just maybe they would understand. They did not. His father was angry and slapped Demetrius across the face but, thankfully, did not resort to excessive violence and just did a lot of yelling. The mom hugged his sister and cried. Then, they made him pray. He was supposed to repent and deny Satan. They wanted him to promise that he would reject moral contamination and sin. What sin? At that time, Demetrius was still a virgin!

His praying lasted for weeks. There were also never-ending sermons. They said that children must obey their parents, that he had to reject his ugly thoughts because men who practice homosexualism cannot inherit God's Kingdom. Sometimes, old men from their church also lectured him. It was all so tiring that Demetrius was tempted to lie and go back in the closet, just to be done with it. But then he remembered what happened to Martin and he stood his ground.

Several months later, they told him that there was a trial in their church and that he was officially expelled. His father called him to the living room. The entire family was there. They announced that he was no longer their son and that he had to leave. They said that it was very painful for them, but there was no other way. Demetrius was allowed to pack a few things, and they showed him the door. His mother would not even give him a hug.

Demetrius was sixteen years old, on the streets, and had nowhere to go. For a few days, he was able to buy some food with the money that one of his sisters secretly put into his pocket. He tried to call his parents, but they hung up. He called his older sister, but she gave the phone to her husband who yelled at Demetrius that if he ever came near their son, he would die. Why on Earth would they think that Demetrius was going to hurt his nephew? He was the sweetest, cutest baby in the world and Demetrius, a proud uncle, loved him with his whole heart! Are homosexuals considered baby killers?

Then, someone told Demetrius to go to that one Chicago intersection because there was a chance that he would find someone willing to take care of him. He did. After maybe fifteen minutes, an older guy driving a fancy car pulled over and took Demetrius to a motel. Demetrius never told anyone what exactly happened in the motel room, but he said that the older guy was a monster who tried to force Demetrius to do unspeakable things. They fought, and somebody called the cops. The guy was arrested, and Demetrius was sent to Longwood, where he spent almost two years. From time to time, he would try to reach out to his parents, but nothing changed. They still would not talk to him.

Demetrius earned his high school diploma and a few weeks later he was discharged from Longwood. He was never heard from again. All he left behind was a drawing. It was a self-portrait: a handsome face of a young man with old, tired eyes, looking into nothingness with an expression of such anguish that it made you want to scream.

CHAPTER ELEVEN

Diagnosis: Damaged Beyond Repair

Some of the boys at Longwood went through experiences so horrible and bizarre that it was a miracle they were alive and functioning at all.

When Tobias was six, for example, his mother killed herself while little Toby was sitting on mom's lap. She accomplished this ambitious goal by blowing her brains out with a nine-millimeter. For some reason, the mom felt compelled to end her life while holding her young son. When he was found, little Toby was covered with his mom's blood and had his mom's brain matter splattered all over his face. He was still holding on to her lifeless body.

Fast forward eleven years and Toby grew up to be a big guy. He was smart, he could be nice, but sometimes he would lock himself inside his permanently wounded mind. Whenever this happened, Tobias was lost to the world. He would not answer questions or make eye contact. He would not move. One day, a bunch of other boys decided to conduct a scientific experiment, and they set Tobias on fire during one of his out-of-body experiences. Tobias did not even blink. The mad scientists were probably even more scared than Toby, and they mercifully extinguished the flames before Tobias got hurt.

When Tobias had a good day, he liked to joke and fool around, and it was possible to have an interesting conversation with him. He would make insightful and surprisingly mature comments. The only topic off-limits was his mother's death, but it was always there, permanently imprinted in his soul. Therefore, from time to time, Tobias would seek refuge in his selective catatonia.

Mike was the physical opposite of Tobias. Tobias was a big African American kid with exceptionally dark skin, while Mike was as white and pale as a Norwegian in early spring. Mike had turned sixteen but he looked twelve. He was painfully thin, as if constantly sick and tired, and he wore thick-rimmed glasses that seemed too heavy for his face. Mike had horrible posture and usually kept his head down. His clothes always looked two sizes too large. Mike was smart and acquired a lot of knowledge in many areas. He was a bookworm, always reading and always lost in some imaginary world. His passion was Greek mythology. Mike knew everything about Greek gods and heroes. He knew all the myths by heart.

Mike was born on a farm that was lost in the middle of cornfields, somewhere in eastern Illinois. His parents did not like him, and they usually kept Mike locked in a chicken coop. Only on rare occasions was Mike allowed inside the house. He was not given regular meals and, most of the time, he was given no food at all. His scars indicated other forms of abuse, but nobody knew much, and Mike was not talking. In general, talking was not Mike's favorite thing unless the conversation had something to do with Greek mythology or the books that he liked. When he did speak, Mike was soft-spoken, polite, and used beautiful, rich language. Mike wanted to become an archeologist.

Recent research shows that multiple personality disorder is real, and Mike had it. From time to time, Mike would turn into someone else. Not only his facial expression but his entire body would change. His voice would become deeper and harsh, and his language was suddenly filled with profanities. Even his accent was different. When this happened, Mike never claimed that he was somebody else, but after it was over, Mike could never remember the episode.

One day, in the middle of summer, Mike went for a walk around the grounds with his PE teacher and one of the paraprofessionals who worked at the school – two young women whom everyone liked. Out of the blue, Mike brutally attacked them. He tried to tear off their clothes and he punched one of the ladies to the ground. He exposed himself and attempted rape. The women managed to escape and summon help. They were both injured and traumatized. They had bite marks. Mike was taken away and never came back.

Markey, however, would never hurt anyone. Markey had autism and moderate mental retardation. His mother left him soon after he was born, and Markey stayed with his grandma, who had no idea what to do with a child with special needs. His grandma did not know that there were resources available to her and to her grandson. She loved Markey and was afraid that the government would take him away.

His grandma had a part-time job and things to do. Whenever she was busy or had to leave, she would chain Markey to a radiator. He did not seem to care. She would feed him every day, but she was not that concerned about his personal hygiene, especially when he was no longer a small child. She never sent him to school. When he was chained, Markey had no access to a bathroom, and his grandma encouraged him to use diapers. They were rarely changed.

One day, Markey got sick. His fever was dangerously high, so grandma took him to the emergency room. The medical personnel immediately noticed the sores; they saw the layers of dirt and called protective services. His grandma lost custody – if she ever had it – and Markey was placed in a residential facility. He was one of the few boys who actually benefited from being at Longwood. While staying there, he was relatively clean and taken care of. For the first time in his life, Markey enjoyed spending time outside. He would touch tree branches and smell leaves of grass with a look of pure delight on his face. His speech improved, he was even able to have a simple conversation, and he made impressive progress at school. Markey remained close with his grandma. He visited her once a month.

While most other boys never left the city, Caleb hated leaving the forest. He was born and raised in the hills of West Virginia. To say that he was raised, as in someone actually raised him, would be an overstatement. In fact, Caleb raised himself. His mother died of natural causes when Caleb was little, and he did not remember her.

Caleb lived in a small cottage with his grandma and his father, but his dad was never home and later moved to Chicago. Grandma was the only caregiver left in the house and Caleb had seven brothers and sister who kept his grandma busy. She also took care of their cousins.

Caleb always liked the forest. He learned how to trap, he hunted with bow and arrows, and he cooked and ate what he killed. He knew how to find shelter and keep himself warm. He understood nature, and he became part of it. While roaming the Appalachian Mountains, he felt happy and free. Caleb did not care much about people. When he was little, he went to school a few times but then decided that school was not for him.

When his grandmother died, Caleb was fourteen. He was sent to Chicago to live with his dad. Two months later, Caleb's father was arrested for armed robbery and went to prison. Caleb was taken by DCFS and sent to a group home.

Caleb had average intelligence, and he was not identified with a disability. Only Caleb, now fifteen-years-old, did not know how to read and write. He did not know the alphabet, and he never learned how to add or subtract. Caleb also did not really know how to talk to people. He had nothing in common with other boys. He stopped smiling, and he was not interested in anything that kept other residents busy or entertained. Caleb did not believe that he could ever catch up with his schooling. He tried to learn how to read but at his age it was hard, so he gave up.

In the confines of a group home, the young Tarzan of West Virginia felt hopelessly trapped.

CHAPTER TWELVE

See No Evil

IDEA (Individuals with Disabilities Education Act) is a federal law that provides services and protection to students with disabilities. All schools that receive public funding must obey the provisions of IDEA. As of today, about six million children who attend American schools receive special education services.

IDEA provides a clear and precise definition of a child with a disability. Determination of a disability must be done through an appropriate evaluation, also defined by IDEA. Only after a child is found eligible for special education services, an IEP (Individualized Education Program) team will design educational strategies that are most suitable for that particular child. The IEP team will meet and decide appropriate goals for the child, related services that the child is going to receive, accommodations and modifications, and support for the school personnel working with the child.

While a draft IEP is often prepared in advance, one thing that must be decided during, and never before, the IEP meeting is the child's educational placement. Federal regulations require that a child with special needs is placed in the least restrictive environment possible. Even if a student has a disability, it does not mean that he or she cannot be taught in a regular classroom with nondisabled peers. The child can be removed from a regular classroom only when the IEP team decides that the severity and nature of his disability justifies the removal.

In case a child with a disability cannot be educated in a regular classroom, the IEP team will discuss the least restrictive environment appropriate for that child. The team must follow what is known as a continuum of alternative placements. Maybe the kid should be removed only for related services, such as speech therapy or social work. Maybe the kid needs a resource room for one or two class periods every day. Perhaps he or she needs to be in a self-contained classroom for most of the day but can have physical education, arts, lunch, and recess with nondisabled peers.

Placing a child in an alternative school is extreme, and IEP teams make this decision only after all less restrictive options have been exhausted, or when the child's disability is truly severe. A student who does fine in a regular classroom cannot be sent to an alternative nonpublic facility just because the IEP team feels like it or because the principal wants the kid out of sight. This would be against the law. Placing a child who has not been identified as a student with special needs in a nonpublic facility for kids with special needs, and then writing an IEP for that child to justify the placement is inconceivable. It is a clear violation of IDEA and therefore very illegal.

In Illinois, group homes and residential facilities that house youth in care of the state for educational purposes belong to the school district in which they are located. Suburban school districts dread the idea of having a group home within their boundaries. Unfortunately, since children in protective services would not magically disappear, some school districts have no choice but to deal with group homes in their midst. Whenever it happens, a convenient approach adopted by many public-school districts is, "Let's pretend they are not here." Many public-school districts do not want youth-in-care in their buildings.

In Longwood, there was a small group of boys with real disabilities. Some sustained traumatic brain injuries, some had intellectual disabilities, some were identified as having speech and language impairment, and a handful had autism. However, the majority of the kids simply suffered from a hard life, which is not a disability category identified by IDEA.

Before being taken by child protective services, most boys at Longwood were general education students and attended regular schools.

In many cases, when a ward of the state is placed in a group home in a suburb of Chicago, he or she is automatically sent to an alternative school for kids with special needs. After he or she is already there, somebody would invent a disability for the child. That somebody would find the child eligible for special education services and write an IEP justifying his or her placement in an alternative school. Here, the order of things, which is defined by federal law, is reversed.

At Longwood, the boy in question would most likely be found eligible for special education services due to emotional disturbance or specific learning disability. The rationale is that a child who is removed from a home and placed in a residential facility is assumed to be emotionally disturbed by the mere fact that it happened. A kid who lived in a dangerous Chicago neighborhood and attended a bad public school, who was hungry and physically abused, would probably be educationally delayed and may show the same behaviors as a student with a legitimate learning disability.

In some cases, a kid would be found eligible under OHI (Other Health Impaired), which could mean anything. It could be we-do-not-want-this-black-gang-banger-in-our-nice-white-suburban-school. For a private child care agency, it could also mean there-is-nothing-wrong-with-the-kid-but-we-want-to-collect-money-paid-for-special-education-in-an-alternative-school.

An assistant principal in a suburban public school asked why she treated a twelve-year-old youth-in-care like a criminal, and why so much effort was put into getting rid of him responded, "Because we must protect OUR children!" A twelve-year-old ward of the state was not viewed as a child, and he was definitely not "ours." He was nobody's, and before he did anything wrong, he was already viewed as a potential threat.

In another suburban school district, Emilio, a high school sophomore who was just placed in a group home for the first time in his life, begged to let him attend a regular school. He always attended regular schools in the past, and he earned good grades. At his first ever IEP meeting, which took place several weeks after he was already placed in an alternative school, Emilio asked to let him go to a regular high school and learn. He begged to at least be able to take a geometry class. The director of special services who represented that public-school district responded, "If you behave, maybe next year I will let you come for PE." That director knew that she just broke a bunch of federal and state laws, but she did not care. Who was going to complain, the kid's parents? In theory, American children have the right to go to school and learn, unless, apparently, they are wards of the state. In their case, public education becomes a privilege that they must earn.

A former principal of a public high school in Chicago said that she understood why regular schools would be reluctant to take youth-in-care and she supported that decision. She said that children and adolescents removed from homes by child protective services would need emotional support that a regular school was not equipped to provide. They would need a smaller class size and constant access to social workers and therapists, which a public school did not have the resources to provide. A youth-in-care would have emotional outbursts that must be dealt with by people with adequate training. In a regular classroom, a child in crisis would not have access to such people. Consequently, he or she would not learn and would also interrupt the learning process of others.

A former youth-in-care disagreed. He said that a kid removed from a home by state protective services should at least have a chance to attend a regular, normal school. Going to a regular school with regular kids would provide him with some normalcy and give him a sense of belonging. A youth-in-care already feels rejected, and he knows that his chances to make it in life are limited. Why slam another door in his face? Educators must not make decisions based on assumptions and prevent a kid from attending a regular school because he may do something terrible or may need something that they are unable to provide. How about letting him attend that regular school with other kids, and move him to an alternative facility only after something actually happens?

In the 2014-15 school year, the total cost of implementing the IDEA was twelve-and-a-half billion dollars[9]. With a possible exception of the Secretary of Education in Trump's administration, Betsy DeVos, American taxpayers never question the need for funding programs and support for children with disabilities. This is because American taxpayers assume that the kids receiving these services are actually disabled. The cost of funding alternative education for the wards of the states that public schools simply do not want to educate is unknown. The general public has no idea that this is happening, and the people in charge who know do not seem to care.

CHAPTER THIRTEEN

How to Torment a Teacher

There are several career options available to special education teachers: most work for public school districts; some choose employment in charter or private schools; there are also a small number of deranged individuals who want to work in the alternative schools, and that category includes residential schools like Lincoln Academy at Longwood.

Lincoln employed four special education teachers, a PE teacher with a general educator's license, and a principal with a background in special education. There were also at least five paraprofessionals to ensure two adult supervisors in each classroom. In a residential school for students with special needs, teachers usually work twelve months a year, as opposed to their public-school counterparts who typically enjoy ten-month employment. In Illinois, residential school teachers work more but make less than public school teachers, although in some states the opposite is true.

Some DCFS residential schools in Illinois have unqualified staff, and others are understaffed or have high school graduates with no credentials teaching core high school classes. Typically, this would not be allowed, and the Illinois State Board of Education would step in to remedy the situation, but for some reason that defies all logic, ISBE has no jurisdiction over DCFS schools. One residential school principal asked why unqualified personnel was explaining to her students an incorrect solution to an equation, responded, "So what? These kids won't know the differences anyway!" In another residential school, an entire semester of high school algebra covered nothing but fantasy football.

However, Lincoln Academy at Longwood was lucky. Most of the time, it was fully staffed, and all teachers held appropriate licenses and came with prior experience.

Lincoln Academy at Longwood was housed in a small, dilapidated building. Two walls were made of cinder blocks with no insulation. In winter, if you left a cup of water in the classroom, the following morning you would find an ice cube. Because the facility was located in the woods, there was always a variety of garden insects crawling everywhere.

The school building had mice as well. Sometimes, students or staff would find a rat, a snake, a turtle, or some other representative of local fauna who would come to school to seek knowledge. On one occasion, the school was even visited by a mink.

There was a long corridor connecting the front and back doors of the school building that lead to multiple classrooms. The hallway was located at the ground level, and after heavy rain, it would completely flood and become impassable. There would be large puddles of standing water, and students and staff alike had to either wade or jump over the puddles to get to their classrooms.

The classrooms were mercifully large and bright, but they were furnished with old desks and chairs that were usually broken. At some point this furniture was brand new and in one piece, but throwing and breaking chairs and desks was one of the students' favorite pastimes, second only to making holes in the interior walls. Outside walls, made of cinder blocks, were immune to physical abuse. The school's bathrooms looked like crime scenes and smelled like decomposing bodies. Nothing in the building was ever clean unless teachers or students decided to scrub it.

Most furniture and other school supplies were brought by staff from the second-hand teacher store, where public school districts donated itemed that they no longer needed and were generally free. From time to time, Lincoln Academy would get new textbooks or other materials and supplies, but these were rare and much-celebrated events. On one occasion, everyone at school was thrilled when a teacher brought boxes with brand new markers, pencils, rulers, and other supplies that were thrown away by a nearby school district and put by a dumpster after the end of their school year.

Although furniture and resources at Lincoln Academy were meager, everyone somehow managed. Teachers were creative and generous with spending their own money. However, there was one time when the students came close to rioting because management ordered another round of budget cuts that resulted in the schools order for clean drinking water to be canceled. The boys were told that they should start drinking tap, but tap water at Lincoln Academy smelled worse than city sewers in Chicago and had the same color as discarded motor oil. However, management explained to the boys that tap water in their school building was safe. After all, they did not have to smell it or admire its color and if they were really thirsty, they would not mind. This ended the water dispute, and after that, no one was thirsty during school hours anymore.

At Lincoln Academy, most teachers, administrators, and support personnel were regularly attacked and injured by students. Some injuries required hospitalization. Many new-hires quit after one day on the job—a few left after only several hours. Lincoln Academy was one of those places that people told horror stories about. To anyone engaged in teaching, it embodies being in trenches. The school's entry door was worthy of a sign, "Abandon all hope, ye who enter here." But was it really that bad?

Lincoln Academy was undoubtedly challenging, but you could get used to it. The boys were not easy to work with but you could grow to love them. You had to deal with their daily shenanigans, you were threatened, offended, you had to duck to avoid being hit by chairs and other unidentified flying objects, you had to deal with occasional rats in your desk drawers, with insects, and with perpetual holes in the walls. Yet, after a while, you would not change this job for anything else.

New personnel at Lincoln Academy, and all new people at Longwood in general, were always tested by the students. The boy's welcoming act was, "Look how bad we are! Are you scared?" If you showed fear, you were done. If you saw villains rather than boys whose childhoods were stolen, you were done. If you were disrespectful, you were done. The boys possessed a superhuman ability to detect behaviors and attitudes that were artificial, and one thing that they hated more than anything else was being lied to — they expected the sincere truth. If you were fake, you were done.

When the boys realized that someone was sincerely invested in helping them, they appreciated it much more than students in a regular school. Those boys took nothing for granted. They would still talk back to you from time to time, put their heads down and refuse to participate, or start a fight, but most of them would at least try to learn.

The teachers who stayed at Lincoln Academy also had other problems. They despised the fact that public schools would never take any of the boys, not even the ones who worked the hardest and showed most progress. They hated the fact that the only choices offered by the transitional program upstairs were watching television, playing board games, or sleeping. They were upset that the boys did not have proper clothes, enough food, or clean water to drink; that they never saw a smart board; that they did not have school supplies they desperately needed. The teachers couldn't stand the fact that the students were denied the right to interact with other kids their age, that they never went on field trips, that they never saw the inside of a theater or a museum, and that their school building looked like something from a horror movie.

Classes were interrupted at least once a day because, somewhere in the building, somebody went into crisis. All staff members were required to carry a radio, and when there was a call for assistance, some would rush to help while others stayed behind in an attempt to maintain the required student to teacher ratio so that a full-blown riot would not erupt. This was so common that after a while everyone knew exactly what to do and where to go. Dealing with a crisis became another routine. A typical school day at Lincoln Academy could look something like this:

- 8:30 am to 8:45 am – Review of previous lesson and a vocabulary exercise.
- 8:45 am to 9:05 am – B.J. punches the wall above the supply cabinet and makes a round hole which is five inches in diameter. Teacher turns it into a learning opportunity and reviews formulas for circumference and area of a circle.
- 9:05 am to 10:00 am – Identifying missing words in sentences using context clues; a group activity.
- 10:00 am to 10:25 am – Marcus throws a chair at Robert in an attempt to cause a severe bodily injury. Robert dodges the flying chair but in the process steps on Juan who is sleeping on the floor.

The educational process at Lincoln Academy was never dull.

CHAPTER FOURTEEN

Cash Cow

Funding for Lincoln Academy was a masterpiece. In general, the tuition for a student with special needs who is placed in an alternative school is paid through tax revenues. The amount changes every year and is also tied to a student's disability, so the tuition rate for a low functioning kid with autism who needs intensive care and a full-time assistant is significantly higher than the rate for a student with a specific learning disability in the area of mathematics.

In Illinois, the average tuition for a kid placed in a nonpublic special education program is around two hundred dollars per day. A school year has approximately 180 days of attendance, and the youth-in-care in residential facilities also attend a summer school, which is adds another 30 days of attendance.

During fifteen years of its existence, Lincoln Academy at Longwood received over twelve million dollars in tuition reimbursements. That would be close to forty-two thousand dollars per student per year, depending on enrollment. This was significantly higher than the average spending per student in an Illinois public school during the same time, and was comparable only to the amount spent in the most affluent public-school districts in the country. Students at Lincoln Academy should have been able to get top of the line instructional materials, equipment, supplies, and everything else. The school should have been able to afford to hire a professional cleaning crew and, if they wanted, one exterminator per every single insect crawling on the walls. The boys should have enough drinking water to fill an Olympic size swimming pool.

All of this could and should have happened, but it did not because, at Longwood, management routinely took large chunks of the tuition money and used it for things that had nothing to do with education. Although this practice was illegal, they were not even trying to hide it. When one of the teachers could not find a single whiteboard marker in the entire building and dared to ask why the school was always struggling and why they were not getting the supplies that they needed to do their job, the management responded, "Because the school cannot keep all that money. You have to share!"

According to federal law, the services provided to a student with special needs stop either when that student graduates from high school, or on the day when he or she turns twenty-two. The second option is meant for young people with more profound disabilities. Even if they meet graduation requirements in terms of academic coursework, they might not have developed the skills that they would need for further education, employment, or independent living. The IEP team would look at a student's transition goals and design the best program for him or her. This may include life skills training, development of vocational skills, and sometimes taking one or two preparatory courses in a community college. The student will probably continue receiving related services, such as occupational therapy or social work.

Although this option is available, most students with special needs do not have to stay in high school beyond the standard four years, and they graduate together with their nondisabled peers. Under no circumstances is a student with special needs kept at school and required to retake classes that he has already passed. Under no condition does a kid come to school only to be placed in a warehouse-type program where he spends his days watching television, playing board games, or sleeping.

High school graduation requirements are based on state guidelines and are slightly different from state to state and from one school district to another. In Illinois, to earn a regular high school diploma, a student is required to earn between twenty-two and twenty-six high school credits, which must include learning specific skills and taking specific subjects.

However, Lincoln Academy was unique. At Lincoln Academy, some students had more than thirty-five high school credits, yet were not allowed to graduate. The management had no functioning transitional or vocational programs. At the same time, they had to do something to keep the residents occupied during the day and at minimum cost. The management also wanted to keep the continuous flow of money that was designated for education, but was routinely used for something else. Therefore, some boys took the same class over and over again regardless of whether they had already passed the class in the previous year, and whether they knew the curriculum by heart. Other boys were warehoused in an empty room where they watched television, slept, or played games. Here, no certified teacher was present.

Almost all boys at Longwood desperately needed to develop independent living skills. Even if they had a home, they usually did not learn much there. They needed to know how to cook, how to wash and iron their clothes, how to clean, how to fix things around the house, and how to sew a button that fell off the dress shirt that they had to wear for an appearance in court. The boys were fully aware of these deficits, and they wanted to learn practical skills. Some even asked to be taught proper etiquette! When deciding what curriculum would be appropriate for courses designated as high school electives, several boys said that they wanted to learn how to act around the Queen of England, in case she invited them for tea. And so, they painstakingly learned which utensil to use with oysters and how to hold a delicate teacup that the teacher brought from her home. They bravely tasted caviar and steak tartare also brought by the teacher, while listening to Vivaldi. For the entire semester, not once would a chair be thrown or a wall punched during a Good Manners Class. For a brief moment, the boys allowed themselves to dream that maybe, just maybe, someday they will be allowed to enter into a different world.

All students at Longwood attended a mandatory summer school. Federal regulations provide an option for an Extended School Year (ESY) when there is a reasonable chance that a student with special needs will forget what he or she has learned during the regular school year. ESY, usually called summer school, is actually different from a summer school for kids without disabilities who simply flunked a class. It is not meant to teach new things. It is intended to prevent forgetting what a student has already learned. Most often, it is approved only for students with more profound disabilities.

At Longwood, summer school was something everyone was required to attend. There were no exceptions. Summer school offered all new subjects with a curriculum not related to what was taught during the regular school year. Summer school at Longwood served two essential purposes: first, it brought in more money—if fifty students attended ESY for thirty days, it would bring in three-hundred thousand dollars; second, it kept the boys occupied without the need to hire additional staff or develop new programs. Lincoln Academy teachers were required to work over the summers anyway and were not compensated with additional salary.

In general, unless a student had to go to court or had an appointment outside the facility, he would be sent to summer school no matter what. This requirement even applied to students who were sick, unless they were too sick to stand without support, in which case they would be taken to a hospital. During school hours, there was no staff available in the residential building where the boys lived. The management had no intention to pay additional salaries. Ergo, if they were able to stand, all boys were expected to be at school.

School personnel had to deal with sick students all the time. When a boy was burning from a fever, staff would create a makeshift bed somewhere in the corner of a room, until one day the management decided that sleeping in the classroom was inappropriate and ordered all mattresses and blankets removed. Sick or not, a student was expected to participate. After that, makeshift beds for the ill were made of several connected desks. In winter, especially during the flu season, staff would even smuggle homemade chicken soup for the boys, although homemade food was not allowed. A sick boy was expected to eat stale bologna sandwiches like everyone else. He was allowed, however, to throw up afterward.

Despite being a cash cow rather than an educational institution, Lincoln Academy functioned remarkably well. Students organized a science fair, they displayed their artwork, and the Math Club worked hard and studied all the time. Members of the etiquette group greeted new arrivals with the phrase, "How do you do? It is a pleasure to make your acquaintance" before beating the crap out of them. And in English, they were engaged in remarkable discussions while reading *Night* by Elie Wiesel, a book describing horrific experiences in Nazi concentration camps. Somehow, these boys understood.

CHAPTER FIFTEEN

The End

The news that DCFS was shutting down Longwood came as a shock. The management must have heard or at least suspected something, but to everyone else it came as a total surprise. An avalanche of wild speculation immediately followed the news: some said that it must be because of the money; that they were misappropriating funds for too long. Did someone in the state government finally realized that Longwood is collecting payments for boys who were not there? That so much of the taxpayers' money is not reaching its intended destination? Others disagreed: it could not be about the money because many private childcare agencies are corrupt, everyone knows it, and nobody cares. It must have been because of the sexual misconduct. Maybe someone reported that the new arrivals, especially the youngest ones, are coerced – or more than coerced – to have sex with the older boys. That sometimes it could be called rape. Or maybe it was something less sensational. Perhaps the management got a better offer and did not want to deal with those teenage outcasts anymore. Perhaps there is a buyer for this whole facility in the woods.

"What are they going to do with us?" All the boys asked themselves this question, but Juan was the one who dared to say it aloud.

The staff members were distressed and not willing to deal with uncertainty among the boys. There were bills to be paid, unemployment claims to be filed, and other jobs to be found and applied for. Management made it clear that they would not be able to rehire any of the employees in a new capacity.

It was a warm, early fall evening and Juan, Tavon, and Mr. R went for a walk around the grounds. "Hey, look," said Juan, "remember when Brody was hiding for hours in that tool shed, and everyone was running around like crazy thinking that he escaped? They even called the cops!"

"And over there, behind that large oak tree, this is where Markey really tried to escape during that blizzard. When they found him, he was frozen solid and barely alive. The idiot was not even wearing his coat."

"Oh, yea," said Tavon. "You bet; I remember. It was after they told him that his grandma died, but they would not even take him to the funeral. Hey, what do you think they are going to do with our hoops? They should give them to someone, so this stuff is not wasted…"

"Do you think they will place some of us together?"

Juan suddenly got angry. "Screw them! Screw them all! I don't need this f…ing place, and I don't care where they send me!"

Later that night, Mr. R found Juan hiding behind the furnace in the mechanical room. Juan was crying like a child. When Mr. R tried to console him, Juan pushed him away. Yes, when you are youth-in-care, getting attached to people comes with a price.

Three weeks later, everyone was gone. Moving the boys out of Longwood was organized swiftly and efficiently. Little time was given for goodbyes and all that sentimental nonsense. If you were separated from the only friends you had in the world, so be it. If you become attached to some staff members, too bad, because you were never going to see them again. Deal with it, or do not deal with it, which is also fine because your new therapist can always extend your sessions and your new shrink can add new meds.

Now, the empty buildings that used to house the Longwood Alternative Treatment Center look like a set from a horror movie. They are as ugly as before, but the eerie silence covers it with a new layer of gloom. In a neglected garden that the boys built behind the school, overgrown vegetation is twisted in a weird angle in a desperate but futile attempt to stay alive. A torn chunk of a screen hangs from a window, but Mr. Bob and his dependable toolbox are nowhere to be found. Even the leaves on the surrounding trees do not dare move. A motionless deer camouflaged in the shrub stares into the void without blinking. The entire compound looks frozen in time, as if the universe itself created a still picture in tribute to the dreams, hopes, misery, and fear that was recently housed here.

Some staff members tried to stay in touch, but the boys disappeared into the web of the residential childcare system overseen by DCFS. DCFS would not say where they moved the kids. Here and there, wherever beds were available and needed to be filled. A few lucky ones went to smaller group homes close to the city. Several were shipped to Kewanee Youth Center or, in fact, a Kewanee juvenile detention center before that one was closed only two years later. All of those closures were accompanied by official reports about beds available, beds lost, and beds to meet the needs. It was always about beds; never about people. It was as if people were not relevant. The boys were just shoved from one bad place to another, each location being a little closer to their final destination: an adult prison where they would end up spending most of the rest of their lives.

A former teacher from Lincoln Academy was looking at a note written by one of the boys: "Sometimes, I wonder why I was born. Do you have an answer that makes sense?"

AUTHOR'S NOTE

I have decided to change the names of some of the people and locations chronicled in this book. The characters described on these pages have suffered enough, and I wanted to spare them any unnecessary embarrassment. When individuals or events became a topic in media reports, I used their original names and provided the information that could be verified.

I spent almost five years at Longwood and left unaware that in just a few months, the facility would be closed. I moved on to what might be described as a rewarding and certainly more profitable career, but Longwood will always have a special place in my heart. Despite the enormous collective baggage carried by its residents, Longwood had something genuine and uniquely rewarding. The boys were exceptionally difficult to work with, but they were also authentic. When you were willing to treat them with respect and show them a little bit of affection, and when you were genuinely invested in helping them, they were grateful, and they would never betray your trust.

I do not believe that a single boy housed at Longwood was a real criminal. Although I am no expert, I do not think that any of those boys exhibited characteristics of a psychopath or a sociopath. They were all scared, abused, neglected, and betrayed, but none of them were actually bad. They were only perceived to be bad by others, especially by the communities where residential housing for juvenile delinquents operates, often depreciating the value of the surrounding properties.

Some of the boys had severe mental problems, they were dangerous to themselves and to others and in desperate need of full-time professional psychiatric care. However, that would be too expensive and the state was not willing to pay. If they are ever released into the general population, God save us all. The rest were just losers in that big lottery called life. They drew the short sticks. Given an opportunity to grow up in a normal home with at least one normal parent, they would be exactly like other kids their age. They acted out because they were very much aware that they held that short stick. They were enraged because they wanted to know, "Why me?"

Some of the people I had the privilege to work with at Longwood were extraordinary. In my long professional career, I have never encountered individuals who would be more committed to helping children. To my former colleagues from the Chicago Bears organization and the Racine Raiders football club – working with you was an honor, and watching your dedication and your discipline has taught me a lot. To the principal of Lincoln Academy, also a former Marine – Sir, Semper Fi defines you. To other dedicated therapists, teachers, residential counselors, support personnel, and maintenance staff – you are the unsung heroes who worked for peanuts with unparalleled tenacity.

To those who took advantage of the boys – I hope you cannot sleep at night.

A couple of former Longwood residents, now young adults, managed to find me and stay in touch. I frequently wonder what happened to the others. I refuse to assume that anyone is in prison and I hope that they all have the good life that they deserve. As to the current and future residents of facilities like Longwood – they have to stop being invisible or undesirable. They were already failed by their parents, and they must not be abandoned by the rest of us.

J. C. Pater

NOTES

1. The study was conducted by the California Evidence-Based Clearinghouse for Child Welfare (CEBC) which was created as a result of collaboration between the California Department of Social Services, Chadwick Center for Children and Families (Rady Children s Hospital, San Diego) and Child and Adolescent Services Research Center. The CEBC was given a task of identifying, selecting and implementing evidence-based child welfare practices in order to improve the safety, permanency and well-being of children and families in the care of the child welfare system. More information on research conducted by CEBS can be accessed through: https://www.ncbi.nlm.nih.gov/pmc/articles/PMC3314708/

2. Chicago Tribune investigative reporters published a series of articles depicting deplorable conditions in group homes for children in care of the state. Articles can be accessed at: http://www.chicagotribune.com/news/watchdog/rtc/ct-youth-treatment-crisis-new-met-20141203-story.html

3. A Miami Herald investigation into Florida juvenile justice system provides analysis of ten years of seldom seen record of various forms of abuses committed on young detainees: http://www.miamiherald.com/news/special-reports/florida-prisons/article176773291.html

4. In 2014, D'Andre Howard was found guilty of a triple homicide in Hoffman Estates, Illinois. The jury took less than two hours to reach the verdict: http://www.chicagotribune.com/suburbs/schaumburg-hoffman-estates/chi-insane-or-great-actor-triple-murder-case-goes-to-jury-20140603-story.html

5. A sixteen-year-old Cory Walgren committed a suicide after being called to the dean's office in Naperville North High School. He was confronted about a video he made of himself having sex with a classmate. Details of the story can be accessed at: https://patch.com/illinois/naperville/suicide-naperville-teen-over-sex-video-highlights-schools-dilemma In January 2019, a federal judge dismissed a lawsuit against the school and the city of Naperville brought by Cory's family: https://www.chicagotribune.com/suburbs/naperville-sun/ct-nvs-suicide-lawsuit-dismissed-naperville-st-0123-story.html

6. Shaquan Allen, a ward of the state who lived at Allendale Association's treatment facility in Lake Villa, Illinois, died following a restraint on March 30, 2016. Allegedly, the boy became combative and two residential counselors tried to escort him back to his room. Since the boy was still fighting, one of the two counselors, James Davis, supposedly placed Shaquan in a chokehold restrain. Shaquan stopped moving and was later pronounced dead at a hospital. https://www.dailyherald.com/article/20160413/news/160419391/

7. The accident took place on January 21, 2013 in Aurora, Illinois. Fifty-seven-year old Theresa Burns, a residential counselor at Northern Illinois Academy, was hit by a car and died while trying to remove an eighteen-year-old girl from the road. The girl was agitated and ran away from the facility into a busy street. https://www.chicagotribune.com/suburbs/aurora-beacon-news/ct-xpm-2013-01-23-ct-met-aurora-hit-and-run-0123-20130123-story.html

8. 2018 Chicago Crime Statistics can be accessed at: https://www.chicagotribune.com/news/local/breaking/ct-chicago-homicides-data-tracker-htmlstory.html . Although the city had fewer murders for the second year in a row, it

was still higher than New York City and Los Angeles combined

9. The EdCentral website provides detailed information on funding IDEA and on distributing grants to the states: http://www.edcentral.org/edcyclopedia/individuals-with-disabilities-education-act-funding-distribution/

Coming soon…

Recycled Childhood

Life and Death in Foster Care

Please, turn this page for a preview.

Foster House of Horrors

In Arkansas, foster parents Richard and Martha Roesch were arrested on charges of child abuse after they allegedly stabbed an adopted kid with a fork and shocked a little girl on her "private parts" with a cattle prod. There were also reports that they were forcing foster kids to wear plastic bags, sleep on tarps on the floor, and use buckets for a bathroom.

In Utah, foster parents Matthew Earl Waldmiller and his wife, Diane, adopted three boys from the child welfare system. They made the boys sleep on the floor in a room without a light bulb and with the only exterior window painted black and screwed shut. The boys, who were between the ages of seven and eleven, were spending close to thirteen hours a day locked in that room. According to news reports[19], when they complained or exhibited behaviors that their foster parents did not approve of, the boys were punished by being forced to eat rice heavily seasoned with salt and cayenne pepper. At times, they were bounded with zip ties or had their mouths and eyes covered with duct tape. At the trial, the couple explained that they felt overwhelmed. While sentencing them to fifteen years of prison, the judge said that they "lacked human decency."

In Wisconsin, Dominique Lindsay was taking care of a foster baby boy, only a few months old. A surveillance camera recorded Dominique yanking the baby from a car seat by his arm and carrying him – also by his arm – across the room. When the baby was taken to a hospital, doctors discovered multiple broken bones and a torn flesh in his mouth. Dominique explained that the kid was getting on her nerves.

For twenty years, the state of New York paid more than one and a half million dollars in child subsidies to an Easter Long Island foster father, Cesar Gonzales-Mugaburu. Once considered a hero of the foster care system, over the years, Gonzales had over one hundred boys under his care. It ended when the state conducted eighteen child abuse investigations against Gonzales who was allegedly sexually abusing the boys, some as young as eight. Suffolk District Attorney, Thomas Spota, commented that "the foster care system in the state of New York is a bureaucratic nightmare."

These cases are not unique. News media are bringing similar reports every day. Children who were neglected and abused and therefore removed from the care of their biological parents are being placed in foster homes where they became subjected to even worse neglect and abuse. Occasionally, atrocities committed in foster homes are so monstrous that they drow national attention.

Few cases were more shocking than the events that took place in the Foster House of Horrors ran by Judith Leekin. The widely publicized story[20] started in Queens, New York, but later moved to Florida where in 2007, the police found a disabled eighteen-year-old girl abandoned in a supermarket. The girl led them to a house of her adoptive mother, Ms. Leekin.

Using different aliases, Judith Leekin fraudulently adopted eleven children with disabilities ranging from autism to blindness. When the police finally entered the house, only ten children and young adults were alive. Eleven-year-old Shane Graham, who suffered from autism, Down's Syndrome, and sickle-cell anemia, vanished without a trace and was presumed dead.

The children were beaten, caged, handcuffed, denied food and access to a toilet, tortured, and threatened with a gun. None was attending school, and only three could read or write. They were locked and forced to spend their lives indoors. They never went to a dentist or a doctor. Those who could talk were telling a story about a little girl with an intellectual disability who was pulling decaying teeth from her mouth. An autistic boy was blind, possibly as a result of never being exposed to natural light. All children were covered with scars and had missing teeth. They were all close to starvation. Their adoptive mother, Judith Leekin, who is now serving a lengthy prison sentence, collected over one-and-a-half million dollars in subsidies from the state of New York. It allowed her to have a lavish lifestyle and move to a beautiful house in Port St. Lucie, Florida. By moving out of New York, she was also able to escape the oversight by the child welfare agencies assigned to watch over her adopted children.

Some say that the foster care system is broken and beyond repair. There are voices that it might be better to return to the old model and put children in orphanages where they will at least be fed and feel safe. Even some of the people who went through the system of foster care agree that it might be the most viable solution. A new face of the child welfare system is that of a fourteen-year-old Naika Venant. After bouncing in and out of the state care and from one foster home to another for ten years, on January 22, 2017, Naika hanged herself in a foster home's bathroom while live-streaming the event on Facebook[21].

Proponents of foster care are aggressively defending the system. There is no going back to the misery and heartbreak from the pages of the Victorian novels. The sheer number of foster homes in the United States dictates the brutal statistical reality that some of them will be bad. If a phenomenon, no matter how horrible, exists in the entire American population, it will also be present in a cross-section of that population representing the foster care. Although sad, it is a statistical reality. Plus, regardless of the occasional horrors, foster care is still the best option for children removed from homes, and it is as close to a family as it gets.

The well-publicized story of Cesar Gonzales-Mugaburu, a foster father from Easter Long Island, had a surprising ending. After five weeks of listening to painful testimony, the jury found him not guilty of abusing the boys. The jurors concluded that there was insufficient evidence to prove his guilt. Cesar's lawyer commented that justice was served. Gonzales walked out of the courtroom a free man. One of the boys who testified for the prosecution, now a young adult, commented that justice was not served.

Nobody will ever know what really happened inside the Easter Long Island foster home. It is easy for a foster parent to accuse foster children of lying. It is equally easy for foster children to accuse a foster parent of abuse. In the meantime, everyone agrees that although it is the best we have to offer, the system of foster care remains a bureaucratic nightmare.

Mike

Sexual abuse of Mike started when he was three. Mike's father was forcing him and his five-year-old brother to do unspeakable things. Sometimes Mike's father participated, but usually, he was just filming and taking pictures. There is a black market for this type of filth, and Mike's father was generating a nice little income. Whenever the boys refused or did not perform to dad's satisfaction, they were beaten, burned with cigarettes, and denied food. With Mike, sexual abuse lasted for over four years.

Eventually, the father went to prison for unrelated crimes and the mother relinquished custody of Mike and his brother. She was heavily addicted to meth and in no shape to care for the kids. Mike became a ward of the state.

He was a sweet-looking white kid with curly reddish hair, dimples, and an arresting smile and finding a foster home for him was easy. But at the age of seven, Mike rarely smiled. And Mike was not adapting well to his new life in foster care. Already a veteran of sexual, physical, and mental abuse, he was exhibiting extreme and sometimes self-destructive behaviors. On two occasions, Mike injured his caregivers with a knife. In one foster home, he deliberately set himself on fire. Running away was the norm.

During the next six years, Mike went through an impressive number of ten foster homes. He was hospitalized multiple times and diagnosed with an entire alphabet soup of disabilities and disorders. Mike had BD, ED, ADHD, PTSD, OCD, ODD, and a few other things with or without acronyms. On top of that, Mike, who as a young child also experienced hunger, was now hoarding food and his foster parents were frequently finding spoiled milk, rotting fruit or putrid snacks hidden in the most unusual places. Mike was receiving all kinds of therapy, but nothing worked.

Despite his inner demons, Mike became a fantastic athlete. He was a tall, strong boy and his schoolmates thought twice before starting a fight with Mike. He tried and excelled in many sports and coaches loved him.

By the end of the seventh grade, Mike was placed in yet another foster home. His new foster parents were Anna and Lester. They lived in a single-family home with their biological son and with Trixie, a huge German shepherd dog.

Before Mike, Anna never had foster kids in her house, and Trixie was one of the reasons. Like all German shepherds, Trixie was fervently devoted to her family and equally skeptical of the rest of the human race. Always ready to protect Anna and her men, Trixie made sure that all other people kept an appropriate distance. If they came too close, Trixie would produce a deep growl and expose her impressive teeth. It was more than enough to keep strangers at bay. Trixie was immensely intelligent, she could read minds, and she definitely understood English, although she did not bother to engage in conversations. If you were brave enough to come closer and look into Trixie's eyes, you would realize that she possessed all secret knowledge of the universe.

When Anna and her husband brought Mike home for the first time, they explained to Trixie that he was now family and therefore should not be eaten. Trixie understood and showed incredible restraint by not growling, however - just in case - exposed some of her teeth. After that, Mike was tolerated and later accepted into the pack.

Anna was determined to change Mike's life. In this troubled and profoundly disturbed boy, Anna saw something exceptional and worth saving. By the end of the first day in her house, Anna discovered that Mike's demons were coming to haunt him at night. Nights were the time when Mike was abused by his father. Nights were setting the stage for fear, anguish, and pain. Mike dreaded darkness. His bedroom had to be brightly lit. It had to be illuminated with intense ceiling light, a nightstand lamp, and a fat rope of LED lights that Mike carried with him from one foster home to another like the most prized possession. The radio had to be on.

In the morning, after the first night in their house, Anna discovered that Mike wet his bed. He also wet his bed the following night and the night after that. At night, this athletic and robust teenager, this fearless Lacrosse player, was reliving his torment. Mike would wail, scream, and sob through his sleep. He was suffering from what is called night terrors, and part of it was wetting his bed. Anna kept changing Mike's sheets every day, but she wanted this bed wetting to stop. Mike was in continuous therapy, he was taking a cocktail of antianxiety medications which would probably put an elephant to sleep, yet nothing seemed to be working. Anna decided to try a different approach. She explained the situation to Trixie and asked her to sleep in Mike's room.

At first, Trixie was not thrilled about the plan. She was not a therapy dog, and she was never trained to deal with people with disabilities. However, Trixie understood the gravity of the task in hand and agreed to leave her usual spot by Anna's side of the bed.

Mike loved having Trixie in his room. When Anna quietly checked on them late at night, Mike was not in bed. He was sleeping on the floor with his hands around Trixie's muscular neck and with his face trustfully resting on her thick coat. Trixie gently raised her head, looked at Anna, and her eyes said, "I got it covered. You may go to bed."

Mike did not wet himself that night or the next. He kept sleeping on the floor, night after night, cuddling with the huge dog. Then, he moved back to his bed with Trixie by his side. His bed wetting stopped. Finally, maybe three weeks later, Trixie decided to return to her old spot in Anna's and Lester's bedroom. She gave Anna that all-knowing look which said, "My job here is done."

Mike never wet his bed again.

Made in the USA
Monee, IL
05 June 2022

97491955R00073